GILES WOOD & MARY KILLEN

COUNTRY LIFE

A story of peaks and troughs

ILLUSTRATIONS BY GILES WOOD

For Godfrey Wood, who gave me a microscope on my eighth birthday

Ebury Spotlight, an imprint of Ebury Publishing
20 Vauxhall Bridge Road
London SW1V 2SA

Ebury Spotlight is part of the Penguin Random House group of companies whose addresses can be found at global. penguinrandomhouse.com

Penguin
Random House
UK

First published by Ebury Spotlight in 2023

www.penguin.co.uk

A CIP catalogue record for this book is available from the British Library

ISBN 9781529900156

Printed and bound in Great Britain by Clays Ltd, Elcograf S.p.A.

Imported into the EEA by Penguin Random House Ireland, Morrison Chambers, 32 Nassau Street, Dublin D02 YH68

MIX
Paper from
responsible sources
FSC
www.fsc.org
FSC® C018179

Penguin Random House is committed to a sustainable future for our business, our readers and our planet. This book is made from Forest Stewardship Council® certified paper.

Contents

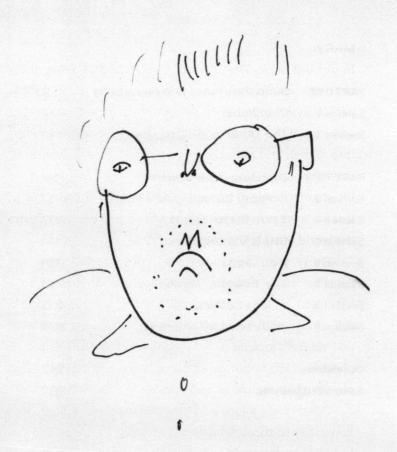

MARY'S PORTRAIT OF GILES, CIRCA 1990

Introduction

MARY:

In our last book, *The Diary of Two Nobodies*, Giles and I charted a year in the lives of two-technically incompatible people living together in a country cottage. One socially ambitious, the other a recluse, 'happiest when staring into a ditch and going slowly downhill', as one old friend observed. Correction: we are not completely incompatible. We share a sense of humour and a taste in friends, but in this book we turn the lens away from ourselves to examine the world outside the cottage window.

Thirty years ago, when we moved to Wiltshire, the decision made financial sense. For the same price as a basement in the outskirts of London, we could have a full cottage with one acre of garden in a beauty spot with real villagers around us – i.e. not weekenders. I would be cheated of the social possibilities of the city, but Giles and our then baby would be far happier.

Others were following suit – it made sense to them too. Especially to those who could exchange a three-bed flat in Islington for an Old Rectory in the country. The trickle became a flood during the pandemic. In the absence of FOMO – no one anywhere was doing anything social or cultural – why not do nothing in the country? Country living, it suddenly became clear, offered a better quality of life – beauty, space, community and health.

Once you could work from home, what did the city offer other than gridlock, where all traffic moves at the pace of a horse and cart, police sirens, parking fines, unaffordable housing and an unnerving atmosphere of transience as though the whole metropolis is one giant airport terminal. And cities are no longer the cultural hubs they were in the days when all artistically aspiring youths were magnetised to the city, where they would meet soulmates and cultural partners. You need money or a rich parent to live in London these days.

Now provincial hubs for artists have come into play all over the country from Faversham, to Bruton, to Frome, to Ludlow, you will find enough 'people' on your wavelength – the new colonisers.

Of course it's nicer to live here, isn't it? Judge for yourself as you read on. Read in the spirit of what it would be like if you were one of our friends and trapped in the cottage with us, listening to us droning on. There will be some stimulating nuggets within the monotony and the – I consider – wonderful testimonies included from 'real' countrymen, indigenae who set the whole life of the incomers into context.

Part One

Despatches from our Previous Lives

PORTMEIRION (DRAWING, PEN AND INK, FROM 1970)

Section 1

CHILDHOOD

On the contrast between
country life in our childhoods
compared to how it is today

GILES:

The Green Comet of 2023 is so rare that woolly mammoths and sabre-toothed tigers were still roaming the Wiltshire plains when it last appeared 50,000 years ago during the age of the Neanderthals.

We were staying with my more successful younger brother who has no street lighting to contend with and so I was able to spot the green fuzzy blob of the comet in the clear skies above his secluded garden.

For thirty years the three street lights in our village have tormented me. But, say some, 'surely you don't object to the new energy-efficient dimmer LED versions?' Well yes, I do actually.

According to my *British Wildlife* magazine the former orange sodium lights were, paradoxically, less damaging to bio-diversity and moths than the new LED ones.

Either way, on return to our grottage, I was forced to walk some distance in the freezing cold to find a spot away from light pollution where I might try to take a second look at the mysterious fuzzy blob then approaching the constellation Camelopardalis.

In some ways, as a malcontent, the Neanderthal age might have suited me, because life would involve only binary choices, such as eat or die — except that I am not a team player which would have meant an even shorter life expectancy. But on the plus side — plenty of bio abundance and at least I could have got through life without medication for high blood pressure caused, in part, by street lighting. Modern life has gotten too darned complicated, and country life is no exception to this rule

Giles, Keele and the Countryside

GILES:

My family lived in Staffordshire, in the rural village of Keele with one shop and one pub, the Sneyd Arms. Keele was then known for its college and now for its university, although halfway through my childhood it would become more famously known for Keele service station.

Our suburban, detached villa, with garage, had metal windows and backed on to farmland. It could be reached by an unmade road so potholes were a feature of my childhood. Residents used to fill them in with clinkers from their fireplaces. There was no protective woodland around it. Consequently there was a wind that howled under the eaves and I remember always being too cold until we got central heating when I was about 12. My sister and I used to put our vests on to rust-coloured Dimplex radiators and steam would rise out of them. My sister was my main play pal. We were only 18 months apart and people often asked, 'Are they twins?'

My late-flowering-lust little brother, Pip, didn't come along till I was eight years old, and I had an abiding image in my mind of seeing him as a babe in arms, being cuddled by my mother, while I was heading off for my first term at a boarding prep school. This guaranteed a resentment that I didn't get over for many years. I am sure I could have been a better brother to him.

In the meantime, in Pip's early childhood, although I can now hardly credit it, I set about trying to have him diagnosed as dyslexic by teaching him the wrong words – pointing to the moon and coaching him to repeat 'duck', for example. He was a splendid little chap but, although there were moments of fondness, it was not until he was an adult at Durham University that I really connected with him as a fully fledged human being rather than as an interloper.

My siblings and I attended a succession of schools but, before we boarded, teatime consisted of my mother bringing out different toasts and Marmite. The toast was always stacked up in a silver dish with a dome on top of it and there was boiling-hot water poured into the bottom of this vessel so the toast was always warm. I remember how delicious it was and how we piled into it. I also remember Shippam's crab and lobster paste, chocolate spread and something called butterscotch whip, which means that nutritionally I was not getting enough of the food I should have got. Chicken was always a treat, which we had at my grandmother's house. She was an anaesthetist at Stoke-on-Trent infirmary and employed a cook and housekeeper.

The field at the rear of our suburban villa had two large ponds which, in winter, would freeze over and my sister and I, along with some village children, would play for hours, skating or sliding on the ice and challenging each other to see how far into the centre we dared go before we heard the sickening crack like thunder.

Sometimes, when the ice was very clear, you could look down and see, as if looking into an aquarium, creatures like the *Dytiscus* – the great diving beetle – and water boatmen, still moving with mysterious purpose in the crystal-clear water below. The more you looked, the more creatures you could identify. It is probable that our attention spans, pre-television, were longer than those of today's children.

Our garden was bordered by a long laurel hedge, which separated us from our neighbours, and we spent hours making dens in this hedge, which seemed to fulfil the primitive need to hide from the world of adults.

It gave security and a sense of familiarity and, at the same time, was a new territory to explore. It was overgrown as a hedge, cavernous, dark and faintly exotic. The 'savannah hypothesis' posited that early man needed a hidey hole from which he could peep out at the world. The laurel hedge meant that as children we lived a troglodytic existence and one of my father Godfrey's earliest terms of endearment was 'Come on, Troglodytes. It's time for your baths.'

As individuals my father called my sister Skinnymalink McCorquodale, while I was known as Trapper Dines because of a character in a childhood book of Godfrey's called *Fur Trade Apprentice*. Stoke-on-Trent had received bombings during the war, and there had been a plan for Godfrey to be sent with other local children to the safety of Canada. To help him acclimatise to the different culture, his prospective hosts had sent across two books. One was *Fur Trade Apprentice* and the other one *The Bobbsey Twins at Big Bear Pond*.

We had an almost Edwardian childhood, playing in the garden, having friends from school over, playing French cricket. One of the things my father was prepared to do was to spend hours with us teaching ball skills. We had endless practice on the back lawn, my sister and I and my father, playing catch with a tennis ball, sometimes playing piggy in the middle. Very simple pleasures – television really hadn't taken over at this stage. It is difficult to imagine a modern father, in our own time-pressured culture, devoting so many hours to such an innocent activity.

Summer evenings were spent playing catch, but not tennis. It was a great regret to him that even though we went to private schools, for some reason neither of us learned to play tennis, which of course is a great social advantage as the skill opens many doors. Years later, when we went to stay in an Austrian *schloss*, when everyone else was playing tennis in the afternoon we felt at a bit of a loose end.

My father rarely missed Wimbledon on the television, but he didn't think that women could ever get to championship quality because their bosoms would hamper their progress. He wouldn't even watch the women's final. He despised football and rugby, although I attended one football match – Stoke City against Coventry City, which my godfather took me to because he wanted me to see the famous goalie Gordon Banks. The only interesting thing to me was that a sheepdog got on to the pitch and held up the match for about ten minutes.

Dens were a thing. And also ornaments. As children we collected ornaments in a way that children don't now.

When we got pocket money our first instinct was to go to buy our parents ornaments. I remember once buying a jasperware Wedgwood ashtray from a 'novelty shop' for my father. It was the highest expression of love and yet I never remember my children behaving in this way towards us.

We had a shed and a metal swing, painted blue, and we could go very high. My older sister, often standing to get more traction, swung much higher than I did but stopped short of doing a full circle.

The garden was not botanically interesting until the time when my mother, who was 22 when I was born, was taken under the wing of an Austrian plantswoman when I was about ten. Together they transformed the quarter-acre into something that was really full of interesting plants and roses. Once she got the gardening 'bug', she effectively gardened the rest of her life away – much to the benefit of insect biodiversity – and in later life she won a wildlife garden conservation award. Fortunately, or unfortunately according to my wife, she spread the bug to me. My mother was an early member of the Soil Association, the campaign group for organic farming and gardening, and this planted the seed of activism in my head and has put me at loggerheads with conventional farmers who are 'not trying to change the world, just making a living' ever since.

One plant in particular fascinated me and engaged the mind with its complexity of shape and colour – this was the bearded iris. The flowers are extraordinarily convoluted and faintly erotic, and it resembles some sort of tropical insect or bird. The bearded iris was in the front garden along with a flowering currant, whose blossom was invaluable to bees early in the season, but which smelled of cat pee. This my mother had inherited along with a laburnum whose popularity in suburban gardens remains a mystery to me.

In the same way, my sister and I found foxgloves infinitely absorbing: we used to peer into the flower heads and then pluck them, and put them on to the ends of our fingers as if they were thimbles. We had no knowledge of how dangerous they could be. Not once were we told to wash our hands after doing this, even though foxglove, along with monkshood, is one of the most deadly of garden plants. Even the laurel hedge in which we had our den was toxic.

Most memorable in the back garden was a huge buddleia near the swing. This was in the days before biodiversity declined, so the buddleia bush in summer would resemble a paisley shawl, so covered would it be with butterflies, mostly Vanessids, i.e. peacocks, tortoiseshells and red admirals, feeding on its blossom. In some hot years, painted ladies would join the throng, floating up from Africa on thermals.

This was when I first became aware of the tongue of the red admiral. We used to try and catch the butterflies in our cupped hands, enjoying the tickling sensation of the wings, and then we would release them. If I added all the time over my life that I have spent releasing trapped insects – bees, spiders, hoverflies, butterflies – it would add up to a significant number of man hours. I also rescue wasps and hornets, knowing their important role in waste disposal.

All our garden plants impressed themselves, in the formative years, and found favour later in my own adult garden because of their scents and the associations with childhood memories.

One favourite trick, endlessly reiterated, was to dig a hole in the garden, cover it with a criss-crossing platform of stems and twigs laid in horizontal fashion, and finished with a light layer of moss or dead leaves. A parent, usually our mother, would then be beckoned towards the pitfall and it never failed to give us satisfaction when they fell in. Cue peals of childish mirth.

Who taught us to make pitfalls? Our parents didn't and there was no learned behaviour from television in those days. I like to fancy that the urge arose from somewhere deep within the onion skins of our subconscious, that it was an atavistic behaviour pattern, a folk memory of the techniques used by our remote ancestors to trap their vertebrate prey. And something that then became purely instinctive – along with our negative reactions to slugs, snakes and spiders.

At each compass point of my universe there were four different family farms. We knew all the surnames, Farmers Twigg, Downes, Summerfield and Locker, but we only knew the Lockers. The potholed track we lived on led to a farm called Highway Lane Farm, which was owned by John Locker Sr, who had a son of my age, John Locker Jr.

John and I played regularly on the farm: climbing up into the loft where they stored grain, jumping on to haystacks and generally having an idyllic childhood.

This was when England had small, mixed, family-owned farms that did both livestock and arable. There was an expression in farming, 'up horn – down corn' and vice versa, so you had the idea that if the cultivated crop did not go well, you would concentrate on livestock. We roamed fields that were mainly pasture and dodged cowpats, or 'country pancakes' as they were called.

Animal manure would keep the ground fertile – this was before the general uptake of artificial fertiliser, which really didn't come in until the seventies as part of the so-called Green Revolution that helped feed the world but was not green in the sense that we understand it today as it was based on huge inputs of newly invented artificial fertilisers, constituting a complete break from thousands of years of using animal manure.

If ever there was a misnomer ...

It was not known then that this cheap food would come at so high a price since fertilisers and other inputs destroy soil structure and organisms, similar to the effect of antibiotics on the human gut.

One of my most vivid memories is of being on a family walk and watching giant machines ripping up the very foundations of the earth as they bulldozed their way through little lines of sportive wood to create the M6 and Keele service station. The peace of centuries was disrupted by the growling and snarling of JCBs – Bamford was a local firm – and later came the constant background drone of traffic, always worse in fog and damp weather.

But before motorway service stations became synonymous with mass culture, they offered a glimpse of a glamorous future. There were also the thrilling childhood moments when our father would sneak us on to the slip road in his Jaguar and we would be elevated towards what felt to us like a Space Age restaurant in which, suspended above the swishing traffic of the new motorway below, we would feast on 'Man Friday's Lunch', which was breaded plaice or cod, chips and peas, as if eating the food of the gods.

Mary, Larne and the Coastal Road

MARY:
Growing up in Larne, Northern Ireland, I don't suppose I had what would be called a country childhood. It was more of a provincial town childhood with access to beautiful countryside but a disinclination to penetrate it. The proper country of the hinterlands was wild, windy and boggy, and, although it was spectacular on the top of the cliffs, with the views on to the Irish Sea – and Scotland could be seen on a clear day – I perceived a melancholy vibe.

Also I had an experience, aged nine, which had turned me off exploring uncharted territory. Two other nine-year-olds and I had set out to have an adventure on the nearby Islandmagee. This was not an island but a sparsely occupied peninsula, parallel to the mainland, and accessible by a boat which made the short crossing on an hourly basis to ferry workmen to the power station on the island. Our adventure had gone disastrously wrong.

I can still picture the three of us on the outward journey, crammed into the open boat in our shorts with our tiny bare legs pressed up against the overalled legs of the workmen. As soon as we docked we ran screaming with excitement towards the first field, which gave a view of the beach beyond it on the other side of the island. Within moments we were waist-deep in a bog and, although we managed to struggle out of it, our shorts, sandals, socks and picnics remained in the bog. To be honest, I can't remember now if the pants came off as well.

In any case, we went straight back on the next ferry to the mainland, our tails between our legs. And after that I wasn't much interested in exploring hinterlands. I had no interest in nature – the only plants I could identify were rose, daisy and nettle, and the only birds robin and seagull.

There was a boat club and the Chaine Memorial Park (donated to the town by a Victorian philanthropist) with acres of greensward, swings and roundabouts, places to shelter from the wind, and a three-mile walkway along the sea where we would duck the waves on high weather days, which fulfilled all my outdoor needs. And then, at 18, I left home and headed for London.

In Larne, I grew up in an Edwardian house bought by my grandfather in 1914. It was a one-off house, built without the help of an architect, but by a builder who obviously had grand designs on his mind. It had eight bedrooms, three bathrooms, assorted outhouses and sat in the middle of a one-acre garden.

Every room had either blazing or wintry sunlight coming into it at some point of the day. There were staggering views of loughs and hills. There was panelling and parquet and fine fireplaces, bay windows and enough assorted box rooms for the grot of ages to be stored out of sight: ice skates, a duck gun, bagatelle, model railways, clothes wringers, hand mincing machines and – a tragic legacy of cruises from the Victorian age – a turtle shell that someone had brought back from some far-flung corner of the Empire. There were two metal larders, out-of-date, smeary cookery books and hundreds of empty cartons from ice cream, which my mother used to store so she could fill the freezer with homegrown raspberries, peas and broad beans.

Our home, called Aranmore, included a surgery where, in the days before health centres, my GP father and his partner, Billy Jamieson, saw patients twice a day.

One mile away was the gateway to the Glens, the Antrim Coast Road, allegedly the most beautiful road in Europe, after the French Corniches, which you could drive along without seeing anything but beauty and majesty – so long as you were going north and looked only to your right. An unfolding panorama of green hills came into view as you turned each corner, each new vista a variation on a theme.

To the left were cliffs rising out of U-shaped glacial valleys, between the cliffs patchwork quilts studded with tiny fields and farmsteads whose boundaries had remained unchanged since medieval times. The coastline was dotted with little shacks and bungalows. As I grew older there arrived bigger, more aspirational houses, but the low-profile man who owned the coastline kept a check on the uglification that has blighted so much of the Province.

My family and I were the co-inheritors of Aranmore when our mother died in 2009 but, although the house was far, far nicer than any of our own grown-up houses, we all now had lives in other places.

We agonised for years over what to do. Should one of us buy the others out and have the opportunity to experience comparatively gracious living near the sea and hills? But this would come at the expense of not seeing any of our friends or family. We no longer knew anyone in Larne and our children had lives in England.

Larne is a seaport 20 miles north of Belfast and 20 miles across the Irish Sea to Scotland. I once met Jeremy Paxman at a party and, when I mentioned I had just flown over from Larne, he expostulated, 'Larne! That's the worst place I've ever been to. Larne?!! What on earth were you doing there?'

Once graced by three Victorian hotels and popular as the gateway to the Antrim Coast Road, the town, which started off so gracious and well proportioned, had over the years become physically ugly.

In the absence of a Larne Preservation Society, all too often an Edwardian or Victorian building that survives demolition will have its fine proportions pulverised, sashes replaced with metal-framed picture windows clad in vertical 'Venetian blinds' or net curtains to conceal the sofa-bound folk within, but let them peep out at passers-by. Brick or stucco walls are refaced with grey, weather-protective pebbledash so that all the buildings resemble police stations. House chimneys where the fireplaces have been blocked up will be sliced off at their bases causing visual jarring as you study those roofs in the landscape.

There was the ubiquitous aroma of coal being burned in open fires, which Giles found overwhelming when he walked in the town. 'Although I have never been to Eastern Europe, I imagine that is the smell of Eastern Europe,' he complained. 'Add to this a huge number of plastic bags which attach to tree branches and you get a picture of a generally unloved town,' he grumbled.

The things that made it special, which any traveller might find characterful, have gone. The hand-painted shop fronts – flesher, gentlemen's outfitters/drapers, ice cream parlour. The shoe shop with orange cellophane wrapping in the windows. Many of these have been replaced by tattoo shops, betting shops, some with cages outside to prevent the windows being kicked in by drunks.

Time was when middle-class do-gooders would have blocked unsympathetic developments but for some reason that stopped happening. The best judges in the world when it comes to music, poetry and writing, the Irish visual taste is what might be called tone blind.

Once, in the eighties boom, valued at a vast sum, Aranmore went on to the market in 2011 but in over five years we had only five viewings of our 'period home'. It seemed there was not a person alive in Larne who wanted to buy it.

'No offence,' said an estate agent. 'I'm sure this place has happy memories for you but young people can't even change a plug.

'They wouldn't want to take on a big place like this with all the restoration work that would be involved – ripping out all the panelling, putting in central heating, picture windows, new streamlined kitchens. They'd have to spend £100,000 on it but you could walk into a property all ready to live in for £250,000.

'More to the point, a house in the centre of a town has no status any more.'

The eight-bed house in its one-acre garden was bought in 2018 by the next door church for a song. We were consoled to think of the rooms being used for prayer meetings or community bonding, or for young offenders to have the chance to learn how to grow vegetables in the gardens, but that didn't happen. The Presbyterian minister didn't want to use it as a manse – he had his manse two miles away and didn't want to live too close to his place of work. Who can blame him?

The upshot was that the church did not get going quickly enough on the restoration and vandals broke in and tried to set fire to it on more than one occasion. They broke a stained glass window on the landing – just out of malice, not because they needed to come through that window – and even though the likely culprits' names were widely circulated, the police, in that provincial way, did not arrest them.

The church said they had no option but to bulldoze the lovely property. It was a dismal ending for a house that had been of such service to both medical and social life – the centre of so many parties given by my parents.

Locals and Exiles

GILES:

The potholed lane we lived on seemed to be inhabited by a gallery of neighbours who were more or less caricatures.

There was the retired Major Richards with his springer spaniel and gruff manner. Having since seen the plays of

Terence Rattigan I now wonder whether he was a bogus military man.

A family we nicknamed the Raggadymen were Irish. The mother was immensely thin like a scarecrow, and all their carrot-haired litter of Raggedychildren were also painfully thin and seemed to have raided the dressing-up box. My sister and I noted that they didn't seem to wear knickers. They appeared to live in a state of bohemian neglect.

There was a woman called Miss Durber, and we made a rhyme about never knocking on her door. *Don't disturb her she's Miss Durber.* My sister and I had a cassette recorder and we would use it to make endless comedy sketches based on our neighbours, interspersed with imitations of the adverts that appeared on the television. We made up one advertising jingle, *Knickerbocker brettels, sitting in the nettles.*

Nearby were squat, brick, Victorian dwellings with allotments. These dwellings remained a complete mystery to us, protected from our curiosity as they were by barking dogs on chains. The people who lived there were the authentic country people, agricultural workers still working on the land, ploughmen, milkers and carters – these by contrast to my father with his villa who commuted to his tile factory in Hanley, Stoke-on-Trent, in his Jaguar, returning home early if it was a nice day to make the most of the sun and his 1960s slatted, woven-plastic recliner. Over his Roman nose he would wear a sunshield, fashioned from the silver paper of his Senior Service cigarettes. He was very good-looking in those days and resembled Roger Moore in his incarnation as

Simon Templar in *The Saint*. People used to stop him to ask for his autograph.

Horace the cowman had the job of rounding up the cows in the field opposite and leading them back through a gate and along the winding lane to the milking parlour in the farm at the end of it. All the while he would shout 'HO-OME' in his deep voice, which echoed behind him in a somehow romantic, rose-tinted way.

He would meanwhile beat the back of the beasts with a switch of elder, reputed amongst country folk to ward off flies. There seemed to be an eternal meaning to him calling his cattle HO-OME as though he were a mythical figure plucked from the fertile plains of the canvases of Poussin or Claude. It was a vision of English pastoralism which was all too soon to be swept away by mechanisation. From my bedroom window I often saw Horace and his mother mushrooming with a wicker basket in the field opposite in the days before fungicides.

All the children in the lane were friends and we played in each other's houses and there were very few restrictions on our freedoms. I don't remember being shouted at very often in my childhood by an adult, but we were scolded for stealing raspberries.

Children used to learn to bicycle by starting on sturdy tricycles and once I had graduated to a bicycle I had a free-range childhood. On my Hercules jeep bike with three-speed Sturmey-Archer gears I could charge along the potholed lanes in all directions, up the dangerous main road for what seemed like miles, even on to the college/university site of Keele with its lakes and land-scaped grounds, in the middle of which was a curious architectural folly consisting of a four-sided tiled building, almost in the Moroccan style.

The base of this folly was filled with channels of water and subterranean patterned tiles, which I became obsessed by because I wanted to know whether, if you fell in, you would drown in one of these passages or come out in some mythical land on the other side. The Rupert Bear comics were full of such outcomes. There were endless underground conveyor belts taking you to different worlds, which came out via the roots of trees.

The rhyming couplets of Rupert Bear annuals were so innocent but almost hippy-like – certainly the ones where they ate blue triangular petals from a flower and suddenly had the gift of flight, although Rupert and Algy always floated on their backs rather than their fronts. They would proceed through a landscape that looked like ours but also had minarets with Chinese professors and talking Pekingese dogs who would be weaving magical spells.

Rupert Bear gave food for fantasists like myself and encouraged me to always note the mysterious and be attracted to the mystic glimmer behind the hills. The illustrator, Alfred Bestall, was almost a visionary of the *Blue Remembered Hills* school of thought. We were proud that the original Rupert Bear author had lived in Colwyn Bay, not far from Conwy, where we had a holiday home.

I know that I frequently cycled far too fast – this was irresistible because of the speedometer that showed my progress and was the must-have bit of gear of the day. There was an all-important top speed of 40, which was never actually achievable. I must have often gone on the wrong side of the road because I was yelled at by motorists. Did I imagine it or were there lorries bearing giant Double Diamond beer cans the size of a tank on their backs?

In those days children would go out for the day and only come home for tea. Their parents would have no idea where they were. We would cycle on our own or with other local children. Unlike me, many of these had mastered the skill of cycling without using their hands. This was an art that astonished me.

We were fascinated by setting fire to things and I once had a box of matches and set fire to the coarse mats of dead grass in the summer. I did this on the verge opposite our house and it must have been a windy day because suddenly the whole of the verge was on fire. Luckily we had Ernest, one of the slabbers in my father's factory, who beat the bank with the back of his shovel to douse the flames, and I was severely ticked off.

Before we got to John Locker's farm there was a massive lump of rock, a gritstone. In your childhood, rocks can take on an animistic, symbolic meaning and on one family walk my father jumped on to it and saluted us: *Guten Tag!* because he had done a spell in the army during National Service and he had spent his time in Germany. And so a large part of our childhood was spent responding to commands issued by Godfrey in German – *Raus!* and *Gehen sie ganzerhei!*

My sister and I treated the stone with reverence ever after. This makes me wonder if the unwearying law of change has somehow miraculously been arrested and if

I were to go back whether I would find what we called 'Daddy's stone' still in its place.

Godfrey was determined to be unlike his own father, who had effectively neglected his children because he was working so hard at the family firm, the tile and fireplace factory, S.A. Wood & Sons of Hanley, to give his sons a higher standard of living. Godfrey's mother had died of an asthma attack when he was nine, in the days before inhalers, so the sons of Stanley Ambrose Wood could have done with seeing more of him. Consequently, Godfrey spent a lot of time with us, going on memorable childhood walks.

Beyond the stone, the lane dipped down to a sinister-looking wood, Dunge Wood, containing a marshy pond with a clanking pump installed, which made a rhythmic noise reminiscent of a chain gang. It was even more sinister when you went into this wood and discovered that there was a railway line at the bottom of it and a tunnel. One of the games we played as children was Dare: daring to go through the tunnel, about 100 yards, and get out the other side before a train came.

There was a fir plantation on John Locker's farm which we called the Thin Wood. This was a steep-sided wood with a stream running through it. We often went to the Thin Wood, where my father and I had once made a very competent and exciting den with hazel lattice, like wattle without the daub. We wove bracken stems for insulation.

One terrible day we found that someone had destroyed it, possibly the landowner himself, Mr Locker, thinking that it might be a shelter for a poacher or a vagrant, then known as tramps. Even then, tramps, some of them shell-shocked soldiers from the war, were a regular feature of the countryside, shuffling along eating raw cabbages from the fields. This gave an early lesson in respecting other people's private property, as my father had not asked permission to build the den and so this was the upshot. Roaming freely over other people's land was one thing, but building a den on it was a step too far.

Once I had taken my teddies Tiggy and Bambi to a hollow oak tree half a mile across the fields towards John Locker's farm. I imagined they might enjoy a night camping, meeting some genuine wild creatures. However, when the weather turned nasty I thought I would go out again and retrieve them from the cavity in the oak tree's roots. As I walked a swirling fog suddenly came down, a real pea-souper, and I became completely disorientated in the fields, not knowing where I was. I was crying my heart out with fear and panic because I couldn't recognise anywhere. Eventually I stumbled into John Locker's farm in tears without my teddy bears, and was driven back to my parents' home in his Land Rover.

But it just goes to show an unimaginable free-range childhood that children simply don't get now. There were no screens to compete with this outdoor life, and farm machinery was less dangerous than it is today. The daytime was for outdoors and people did not live indoors as they do today.

MARY:

The people of Larne are, or at least *were*, the nicest I have ever met. I remember their honest, merry, friendly, kind and decent faces so well. And I remember Larne people's descriptive powers, their beadiness of observation and their wit. Just naturally witty – all of them. Even the dour Presbyterians.

When the Celtic Tiger thing came to an end in 2008, one southern Irishwoman, responding to the news that the party was over, said on Teilefís Éireann, 'Well we won't have the helicopters or the champagne any more but sure we've always had our music and our talk and we'll still have them.'

'Crack,' Giles likes to say every so often. 'Spelt CRAIC.'

'No,' I insist. 'They have craic in the south but not in the north.'

Whether it is north or south, the talk is really where the Irish come into their own.

In England, it seems to me that all too often when you deconstruct a conversation you have had at a dinner party, you will find it was all about establishing status or extracting useful networking tips. In Ireland, it's all about *entertaining* your interlocutor, usually by conveying a truth in humorous manner.

I just don't know if it's the same today as it was when I was growing up, but I would say that any one of my parents' friends (they had about 30 – there was no friend inflation in those days) could go on television and talk, like one of Alan Bennett's *Talking Heads*, and you would be fully entertained.

One of the things that had struck my mother as terribly unjust was that my grandfather, also a GP in Larne, was so devoted to his calling that he very often didn't charge his patients – knowing they couldn't pay. Some of them notched up large debts with him.

Then the National Health Service came in during 1948 and everyone was told they would have free medical treatment. All they had to do was sign up with one doctor and go on to 'his panel' – all doctors were men in those days. That doctor would then be able to keep the patient's medical records and keep a chart of their progress.

Well, my grandfather was 68 and so, assuming he would be retiring soon anyway, very few patients signed up with him because they didn't have the gall to go in and register on his panel without first settling their bills.

My mother viewed the whole thing as an *X Factor*-type popularity contest and was shocked that the public flocked to the new young upstart doctor who had committed the solecism of having a brass plaque advertising his services outside his house. In those days that was thought pushy in medical circles.

My grandfather, indisputably the most revered and the best of all the doctors in the town (he was also a surgeon), was not at all upset by appearing to fail the 'popularity' contest. He was just sorry for his poor former patients, knowing their consciences would trouble them, but my mother thought it 'very mean of them'.

Why am I going through all this? Well because, as I think of all the history of my family's house and the morally distinguished antecedents of my own who lived and breathed in it, and all the townspeople who came in and out of the house, and the garden and all the hours of work over a hundred years that went into it – the rose bushes, the raspberries ('Scottish and Northern Irish people', notes Giles, 'are the only people who pronounce the P in raspberry'), the bird baths, the lawns, the stone steps to the front door – the hundreds of times members of my own biological family looked out through the same windows, walked on the same parquet, shut the same heavy doors, listened to the wind whistling around the same corners and saw the same people made up of roughly the same biological ingredients as our own, speaking in the same accents, walking past the house, informed by the same beliefs and by the same culture, it felt like cutting off a limb to let this family house go.

But would I be living in Larne mainly in order to conflate myself with distinguished antecedents and remind myself that, even though I might be lazy and pretentious and untidy myself, at least I had in my DNA really good people and I could aspire to being more like them as I moved through their shades?

I have no connection with Wiltshire, after all, other than that I've lived here for 30 years. And the Wiltshire natives have no reason to feel any cultural or historical connection with us.

If, by contrast, I moved back to Larne, I would be mixing amongst people with chilblainy complexions and burst veins and puddle-coloured hair like my own, people who had been frightened by the same men of violence and who had gloried in the same stretch of coastline and the tiny fields in the hinterlands and who had listened to the same music and mourned the same victims and had ancestors lying in the same graveyards as my ancestors.

'And no doubt your ancestors also ate dulse, the local seaweed,' interjects Giles.

'I'm sure they didn't. It was too salty,' I reply.

Would it be a good thing to go back? Would it make me feel more at home? I think it was Noam Chomsky who said that no one ever really feels at home unless the language spoken around them has the same nuances and meanings as it did when they were a small child. Therefore you might grow up in London, then move to New York, but even though you had a better life – materially and stimulation-wise – you would always feel that the radio had not been quite tuned while you were in New York and only feel 'right' when back in London, even if in lesser circumstances.

Or, I wondered when contemplating whether to sell our Irish house or not, would I feel, were I to go back and live in it – buying my family's share, selling my cottage and living off the difference until death – that I was a double exile? Who would want to talk to me about smart literary people or artists or about Jamaica or about English politicians? I would feel either patronising or patronised.

I remember watching a sad programme about people going back to Jamaica after 40 years of longing to return to their homeland. But instead of being celebrated on their return, they were cold-shouldered by those stay-behinds who hadn't gone abroad because the returnees made them feel they'd missed out on something interesting. They – usually wrongly – perceived the returnees as swanking over their contemporaries, who had once been their financial equals.

Locals Versus Incomers

GILES:

The only sinister thing I can remember from my country childhood was the time when my 11-year-old sister had a 13-year-old friend who had matured early and used to like going to a transport café off the main trunk road near Madeley to flirt with men, specifically lorry drivers. My sister was a willing companion.

When she found out, my mother forbade my sister from ever going to the transport café again. She didn't explain why, but this was the first sense we had that there was any danger from either strangers or adults.

Apart from the Moors Murders (which we knew nothing about), it would take decades before Stranger Danger became a widespread worry. As the author John Michell has elegantly expressed it: 'it was the demon of sex obsession which has made it unusual or difficult for an adult to befriend a child in the spirit of Silas Marner'. There was a long history of adults and children being charmed by each other and yet now it is illegal to even take a photograph of a child unless it's your own.

I was a middle-class boy who was sent away to prep school at the age of nine. One day as John Locker Jr and I walked to the Thin Wood, we were joined by a local 'snarget', a word coined by *Stig of the Dump* author Clive King. Snarget in Clive King's parlance equalled a 'hooligan' or today's yob.

In the very stratified world which I grew up in – where

there were three distinct classes as lampooned by John Cleese, Ronnie Barker and Ronnie Corbett: Upper, Middle and Working ('I look up to him ... but I look down on him') – I simply didn't come across snargets in the normal run of things.

That day we met up with this snarget, who was roughly our own age, he decided to join us on our walk. He was practically feral and one of the things he did, which shocked me, was that he threw sticks into a tree and dislodged a wood pigeon's nest, which was full of fledglings.

The nest seemed to float down like a parachute and landed upright on a piece of turf on the forest ferny floor.

It had a soft landing but the fledglings were gulping. What happened next made me feel like retching. I had so far lived in a U-certificate world. The only frightening thing that had ever happened to me before this was that once, when we went for a walk on a hill in Wales led by my father, who thought the whole countryside was his personal fiefdom, an angry woman brandishing a stick ran towards us shouting that we were trespassing. My father told us, 'Don't worry – she is obviously a simpleton,' and, sure enough, she was soon called to heel by a minder.

The snarget stamped on the nest with his great hobnailed boots and the fledglings were obviously no more. This was my first X-rated experience and coincidentally an introduction to the sort of savagery that is merely part and parcel of life amongst real country people – the sort who make their living in the countryside.

It may have seemed to me that this boy was almost feral, but there is an argument that 'true countrymen' are not so far removed from the hunter-gatherers of the Mesolithic period. They have a non-sentimental view of life – an us-or-them mentality and a utilitarian view of livestock.

You read of these utilitarians in Spain where, if a donkey is no longer of any service to his master, rather than have it put down by a vet, they will push it into a ravine. You heard of them when the island of St Kilda was evacuated in the 1920s and the men unabashedly drowned their faithful collies, loyal companions of their lifetimes, one by one, before boarding the evacuation boat, since the collies would be no use to them on the mainland.

But it would be wrong to think that this attitude prevails amongst livestock farmers because during foot-and-mouth and avian flu crises, you come to realise, although the animals will all end up in a slaughterhouse anyway, how much of a bond there is between animals and those who handle them.

John Locker Jr was a country lad too – so he said nothing. The fledgling incident was brutality that I had never seen before and so beyond the comprehension of a child brought up in the anthropomorphic world of Beatrix Potter, Pooh Bear and *Wind in the Willows*. It was like being shown your first video nasty, as I was a boy who used to rescue fledgling birds and keep them alive with straws.

At my prep school there was a boy who attempted to revive dead creatures with an Eveready battery and a copper wire because, even then, the Frankenstein myth had taken root in the minds of small boys.

I said nothing either. I looked away, I didn't plead with the snarget to behave in a middle-class way, nor did I show any emotion.

It is easy to forget that almost everything we call wildlife now was persecuted to near extinction until the Wildlife and Countryside Act of 1981, and country boys in the early part of the 20th century would openly count 'bird-nesting' as a favourite hobby. This was the robbing of nests for the novelty of collecting the pretty eggs as specimens, and also there was a fair amount of mischief-making and destruction which came with the territory.

'Oby and His System: The Moucher's Calendar', an essay by 19th century Wiltshire nature writer Richard Jefferies, described how the same man who deftly picks watercress to sell to householders in the towns, also lines his pockets with birds' nests still full of eggs – for no other reason than to remind the townsfolk of the countryside and its beauties. In those days there was no precipitously steep decline in wild birds – this has only happened in the last 30 years.

I did get an air rifle when I was about 12 and, having loved garden birds, I myself then started shooting them with an air rifle. According to the old school this behaviour would be a very natural feature of adolescence. It was considered a rite of passage that you would graduate from a catapult to an air rifle.

I am not proud of my short-lived cruel streak. But at the time I wanted to show my skill in downing small birds, starlings, wood pigeons, and I even shot a blackbird in my garden. Almost as soon as I had done it, I regretted it. It is just a stage of beastliness that boys go through.

In those days shooting birds would have been almost encouraged by post-war fathers whose greatest fear at the time was that they would see any sign of effeminacy in their sons. Then society was judgemental and the sexes were very regimented. For a girl, a present would be a crochet set, a doll, a doll's house, a toy brush and pan. A birthday present for a boy would be a small sailing boat, a carpentry set, a bicycle, a chemistry set. Books would be about alpha males; Robin Hood, Robinson Crusoe, Huckleberry Finn. It was 50 years before *Billy Elliot*.

This is a key point: the difference between the indigenous country folk who live *off* the land and the country folk who don't live off it, just *on* it – who live on it for the view, the space and the privacy. We don't even know what the crops are until they sprout.

Later on in life, one of my own children asked an elder in our current village what she should do with some fledglings, which had fallen out of their nest and which she had put inside her hat. He said, 'What I do with them is that I throw them against the cottage wall. Mother won't go back to them now once she smells humans on them, so they'll just die. Best to finish them off now.'

I thought it was a churlish thing to say to a little girl. But this blunt elder would have been brought up at a time when he would have been familiar with the gamekeeper's gibbet, where the gamekeepers used to hang magpies, stoats or jays to discourage others from the same species. He would not even know what sentimentality was.

There was another story of when I rescued a foxhound up on the downs. He was lost, dazed and confused and injured, and, as a herd animal, reluctant to respond to a strange human. I returned with a wheelbarrow, and coaxed him towards me and wheeled him back down to the village where I returned him to Ted, the huntsman, and he thanked me ... but not effusively. He said, 'I have seen much worse than this. I have seen foxhounds with the flesh hanging off their bones.'

It seemed he was doing his best to educate this townie about just how brutal *real life* is. People who came into villages like us in the eighties were called yuppies, and I wondered if he was thinking, *Give the yup a blood-curdling tale to tell his friends at one of their dinner parties.*

By the same token John Peters, a tree feller from down in Devon who I know, has relished telling me blood-curdling tales of what can happen in the world of the chainsaw wielders.

One man John knew climbed to the top of a ladder to fell a fractured branch. The chainsaw blade encountered a knot in the branch, kicked back and got the man in the jugular.

He was found later, still in the tree, his head slumped, dead.

The reason that John Peters mentioned him was that his widow had recently donated this same chainsaw to John, but he was wary of using it as it had not been used since it killed the man. The idea that an inanimate object could be 'haunted' in this way was almost an example of contagious magic out of the pages of Frazer's *The Golden Bough*.

Closer to home, as our own local tree feller Andy is working in my garden he likes nothing more than to talk about the veteran trees that he has had to fell in the nearby Savernake Forest. Some of these he described as 'widow makers' because, even if you follow all the safety instructions in the world, trees have a way of getting back at you. Elm trees in particular had a reputation of killing those who sat underneath them, by suddenly dropping boughs on to them.

Ellum she hateth mankind, and waiteth
Till every gust be laid,
To drop a limb on the head of him
That anyway trusts her shade

RUDYARD KIPLING, FROM 'A TREE SONG'

Later, the same plain-speaking elder used to sound his horn each time he passed our cottage. This was following a run-in, or minor tiff, I'd had with him on a country walk where I was technically trespassing in a rape field while looking for butterflies and he decided to 'call me out' for it. Words were spoken.

With the horn blowing he was harking back to a folk memory of the country tradition of the 'Rough Band', a country way of signalling that, within the community, someone had done something bad or beyond the pale. It was still in action in the mid-20th century and was chillingly described by George Ewart Evans in *The Pattern Under the Plough*.

Villagers would bang pots and pans and blow whistles. They would go to the house of the wrongdoer and make a racket and a din, and no doubt throw stones at the windows. Our elder's horn sounding was vaguely disturbing, yet interesting as it was linked to the Rough

Band tradition. But of course I could never discuss the finer points of oral history in rural Suffolk with him as we did not have that sort of relationship.

This and the snarget incident were representative of the ongoing country battle of locals versus incomers/ middle-class villa dwellers. We lived in a suburban villa, part of the infill on a country lane – it should never have been built. Our world was at odds with the red-in-tooth-and-claw reality of their more natural world.

These themes reappeared in *The Siege of Trencher's Farm* by Scottish author Gordon Williams, in which a rural incomer comes to a distrustful closed community, with all the potential for disharmony, which became the celebrated *Straw Dogs* film of 1971 with Dustin Hoffman and Susan George, directed by Sam Peckinpah.

Missing Ireland

MARY:

As a child my mother would make me wait at the window when the coal and anthracite delivery men came. They were almost Dickensian, black with dirt from head to toe with leather aprons and leather knee-protectors.

They carried the bags of coal on their backs, one by one, but because it was so difficult after they had gone to judge how many sacks they had thrown in, my mother would post me at the surgery corridor window to count the bags so they couldn't cheat us. I stopped concentrating after about bag three but the coal men didn't know that.

Then there was the funeral 'yard' next door to the back of the house. John McConnell ran it. It was an L-shape made of one-storey buildings with wooden walls and corrugated roofs, all painted black. In the corner of the yard was a little office in which sat Maureen McLarnon, sister of the famous local artist Sam, who could knock out a watercolour a day. Maureen had jet-black hair, a white face and red lips, a round-necked jumper with pearls and a tweed skirt.

Every so often we heard a deafening hush, which was the signal to bring down the blinds in the kitchen looking on to the funeral yard. Our cleaner Mrs Mac adored a funeral day and plotted her time so she would be washing up at the sink while the mourners were awaiting the departure of the coffin from the morgue, and she could peep through the blinds.

All the men smoked. There were no women. Then the coffin was brought out and into the hearse and then it proceeded at 4 miles an hour uphill to the cemetery at the top of the town, the surviving men walking grimly behind it to show respect. The men all had character etched into their faces, partly from groaning as they heaved things in their line of work and domestic life, and partly from facing into biting winds as many had worked outdoors.

Out of the front window I could see weddings, funerals and christenings taking place in the church next door and always on Sundays the intrusive clockwork gong going for 15 minutes as pillars of Presbyterian probity filed into the church wearing solemn expressions.

I was made to do homework in the kitchen while my parents watched television. It was an inefficient scheme to get the best out of me. I just sat in the kitchen and looked out of the window. Because we were so convenient to the centre of the town, my age group of boys started assembling outside, knowing I was in the kitchen behind the blinds, and that no one could see their approach. I didn't do any work, I just ate biscuits, and every so often my mother Betty would rage into the kitchen saying I hadn't put the lids back on the tins and as a result the contents would go off.

Given how domestically annoying I was in early life, I have fully deserved the karmic consequences of being annoyed myself later on in my own home.

What my mother should have done, of course, was to make me sit in the same room as her and my father Tim – doing the homework even if the television was on. Or she should have put me in the little study at the front of the house to do it at a desk. But trying to do it in the kitchen with all the fridge noise and the boys grouping outside the window and the biscuit temptations ... Of course Betty herself had a will of iron. How could she know that her daughter was so easily distracted?

Betty was a productive gardener and something of an athlete as a by-product of being so. When I was 21 she asked me to go and dig up some potatoes from the top garden. I didn't have the strength in my arms. Exasperatedly she came up and did it herself. Playing bridge, growing vegetables and digging potatoes kept her active till the age of 90, but she was always a very practical person and, with all her friends dead, she reflected that 90 years were long enough to live for and she managed to die then herself.

Meanwhile the town had changed from *circa* 1946, when Betty first arrived there for a summer holiday at the sea, invited by my father who was a medical student at Trinity College, Dublin, while she worked in admin at the Guinness factory there.

What changed the lovely place where people could go on holiday without locking their doors was that an English magnate built a factory there in the seventies.

He put out a call for workers saying that anyone in the whole Province who had never had a job before, who had always been rejected from any job they had applied for could come to the town where they would find a job at the AEI factory in Larne. Houses were thrown up in a new district called Craigy Hill, which was built to accommodate these deracinated incomers. One thousand five hundred people came in. Serially people were let go and then the factory closed altogether in 1991.

And then there were the Troubles starting in 1968. When growing up I remember someone saying on television, 'We have a lovely wee country here without wars.' Larne was not so bad because the percentages of Catholics and Protestants were not concentrated together. But it was still so sad that a place that had been so friendly became a place where masked men would stop you at night in pop-up roadblocks – in a sort of self-appointed vigilantism.

When he first came to visit in the 1980s, Giles was very shocked that you couldn't just drive into the town centre and nip into a shop without leaving another passenger in the car (in case you had left a bomb in it). Giles also kept wearing a Barbour despite its associations with off-duty army officers.

As a child, I thought of all the advantages we had, not least the lack of savagery and the prevailing ethos of kindness and decency, to say nothing of the natural beauty around us. I used to think, *Northern Ireland has got to be the best place in the world.* And by 14 I had been to France and Germany so I knew a bit.

But towns in general looked more aesthetically pleasing in the past (a different calibre of person was in charge of planning legislation). And the Larne locals were not only entertaining conversationalists. As a teenager, you could hitch-hike, as I did, in a miniskirt, slightly drunk, without fear of molestation or abduction. There was no crime in Larne. Correction: there were two criminals. One was a child molester, who every so often would come out of jail and our parents would tell us not to go near him. The other was in the Petty Sessions once a month for having urinated in a shop doorway.

And suddenly overnight people in Larne turned against each other, and cruelty and fear began to predominate. I went back often and sometimes for many weeks at a time, England became my home. Not least because of the terrifying Troubles.

So, going back to imagining myself in that kitchen now if I had conjured up the money to keep the house: I would go in there to make toast of Irish soda bread or wheaten bread and Punjana tea. I would be listening to Radio Ulster or Raidió Teilifís Éireann and I would be hearing the voices of people on my own wavelength.

So much is simply understood and there is no need to spell things out. It is just accepted that this is the way things are in Ireland and no one needs to explain anything.

Once while sorting through the plates in our kitchen, after our mother's death, I listened to *Liveline with Joe Duffy*, a talk show on Radio Éireann.

A woman called Bridget rang in and said something along the following lines:

Bridget: De odder day, Joe, I broke down in my car when I was going tru Blanchardstown and dis very nice fellow stopped and started it again for me. And when I got home, I looked in de back seat and dere was a jacket, and all the keys to de man's own car, a Volvo, and I wonder would you put out a call for him to tell him to get in touch because I've no idea what his name is so I can't return the tings to him.

Joe: Oi will. When did dis happen Brigit?

Bridget: Oh it was last Tursday.

Joe: Could you not have called in earlier?

Bridget: Sure I should have done but I taught he might call into you.

Joe: Can you describe him?

Bridget: No, but you'd know him. He was a terribly decent fellow. Oh and he was wearing a Rathgar rugby club shirt

...

[Fifteen minutes later, Bernard, the Good Samaritan, rang in to claim his jacket and keys.]

Joe: Were you not angry with Bridget when she drove away with your car keys? Sure a new set for a Volvo would set you back a couple of hundred?

Bernard: Ah no. Sure I thought I'd just wait until she rang in to you.

Joe: And we got some more good news. A hotel in Rathconan has rung in to offer you, Bernard, two nights' free accommodation to thank you for being a Good Samaritan.

That call encapsulated everything I miss about Ireland. The smaller more manageably sized community where everyone knows precisely what you are like so you waste no time being pretentious. Your status is not linked to class or money but to how decent a fellow you are. Ireland was a ratings-driven community. Unlike Airbnb and Uber the ratings were not delivered online but communicated verbally and facially when two were talking in real life together.

'Do you know so and so?'

'I do, ah ...' And just the way the word 'ah' is pronounced would be enough to say it all.

Nature and Interlopers

GILES:

I had the smallest room in the house, a tiny little 'slit of a room', which may have had a subtle effect on me in reducing my ambitions and life expectations. This may be why I am attracted to the Tiny House movement whose subscribers aspire to own less to live more, occupy less space, learn to tread more lightly on the earth.

My tiny childhood bedroom may have been the reason why I bought a tiny cottage in Essex – apart from the fact that it was all I could afford and I had no visible means of support in those days, except a very spasmodic career as a landscape artist.

A carpenter had come in and built a bed for me, which rested on a flat cupboard which was like a locker for my toys. The room overlooked the front garden, which I liked because I could see anyone coming up to the front door. Because I spent so long looking out of the window there was an incident where I noticed my next-door neighbour's wife being taken out of the house in a coffin. This was my first brush with human mortality.

I began to notice birds in the front garden and I looked at them through my father's Zeiss army binoculars. They were great tits and blue tits but it seemed to me that they could easily have been called yellow tits because the biggest area of colour was yellow. I was completely enchanted by them.

Once I started noticing birds I became an absolute fanatic, identifying all the garden birds and getting books on birds, most of which I still own now. The best book, despite being in black and white, was very thorough and allowed me to identify all the garden birds. I started drawing them in notebooks and Godfrey encouraged me to keep a bird diary.

Godfrey also bought me a microscope and I could look at pond life such as microscopic single-cell organisms at a magnification of 300 so I could see in great detail *Daphnia* or water fleas, volvox, a genus of green algae, and a slug-like filament-type creature called *Euglena*, which had both a repellent appearance and a repellent name.

Mary and I have found that one of the few things we have in common is a dislike of horrisonant i.e. ugly-sounding words, of which we put *Hainault* joint-first with *tilth*.

I went then through a scientific stage and did drawings of all these creatures, partly to impress my father but partly because it seemed that as a budding naturalist this was the correct scholarly and studious thing to do.

My father was very proud that I had kept a Charles Darwin-style exercise book to log my findings, soft-backed with lined paper. E.O. Wilson said that the way to make a naturalist for life is to harness the child's curiosity when young – something I have signally failed to do with my own children. It is interesting that Elgar, towards the end of his life, also had a microscope and looked at microscopic creatures.

If you are not interested in weeds and bugs, which is to describe these things at their most basic, then you might not be able to sustain enough interest in the countryside to make it worth your while moving there. And you will live the sort of detached fidgety life that many incomers do, going back and forth to London. It's a mistake to come to the country only for space and privacy. You must have an interest in some form of wildlife, or in growing things; it's not enough to be interested just in the birds that you feed on your bird feeder.

Only last summer we visited a couple living in a spaceship-type property, which looked as though it had just landed in about five acres of well-mown lawn. They were proud of the expanse of 'mild' scenery around them and had no desire to drill down into a more granular or cellular reality.

I am also thinking of the tech giants who bought a farm in Oxfordshire. They were third-generation city folk with no knowledge or interest in birds and bees. They subcontracted the farming bit of their acreage and had a garden centre in to design a garden for them – which is a bit like getting Walmart to design a garden centre. They understood the lure of the countryside, which for them was the luxury of owning acres of land, but nothing of the *lore* of it.

They were in the vanguard of a new class of landowner who buys a farm, not to farm it, but for the privacy and protection that owning lots of land affords – particularly in the West Country where dairy farming is a marginal activity anyway. Many of these farms have been turned over to equestrian interests with concomitant disfiguring jumps made from tractor tyres, barrels, temporary enclosures marked out with ticker tape. Horses are not necessarily a good thing for biodiversity.

There is a tax advantage to buying a farm as you can pass it on to a child without the same penalties. There were also, up until recently, generous grants from the EU for very basic payments such as stewardship schemes and minimal amounts of action had to be taken by the 'farmers' to 'qualify' for these.

'How else am I going to be able to afford two sets of school fees?' one local landowning wag said while laughing at a Devon dinner party.

'Farmers' today often don't know the names of their fields. The indigenous population of our current village knows all the names of the fields around here. If you are trying to describe a landscape to someone, it is quite difficult if they are a newcomer. 'We were coming down the hill the wiggly way.'

In Keele our back garden had a white picket gate through which we went to roam through a larger acreage of rolling pastureland. In the middle of the field behind our back garden was a huge ash tree in which my sister fancied that she could see the shape of 'a baby with a bonnet' nestling in amongst the branches. In those days there were still flocks of lapwings, or peewits as they are known in some counties.

What would be very interesting is to go back to Keele now and see if that ash tree had died back or been swept away as a part of agricultural intensification where fields are ploughed up and field trees are felled to make way for cereal crops with ever bigger machinery as farmers grapple with economies of scale. The bigger your 'unit' the more efficient the farming can be in producing yet another commodity that can be traded on international money markets just like iron ore or tin.

MARY:

I have sympathy for the hard-working farmers, however. Without them the whole place could be easily be concreted over or blighted by wind farms. In conversation with farmers I have never succeeded in getting a satisfactory answer to the question of why flax and sunflowers (which sell at £3 a stem on the Fulham Road) are not widely grown. But I suppose that those who question me as to why the cottage is still unfinished after 30 years have equally failed to achieve a satisfactory answer.

Childhood Books

GILES:

We were brought up on *Babar the Elephant, Winnie the Pooh, Swallows and Amazons* and Beatrix Potter, although my father was much more enchanted by A.A. Milne's *Now We Are Six*. This is when we were introduced to the idea of paving in London and how, if you trod on one of the lines, a bear would come up and eat you. We read all that sort of pre-Shirley Hughes, pre-topical children's literature. No children's author had tackled gritty subjects in those days – the most gritty children's writer was Arthur Ransome. And of course Richmal Crompton and Enid Blyton. I do believe that I enjoyed the golden age of children's literature. *Mistress Masham's Repose* by T.H. White, *Songberd's Grove*, *Castaway Christmas* – was there ever a better time to be a child or adolescent discovering the magical worlds of Alan Garner in *The Weirdstone of Brisingamen* and *The Moon of Gomrath*, which were like primers to Tolkien's magnum opus *The Hobbit* and *The Lord of the Rings*? Within pages of Garner, the children were being kidnapped and pinched by goblins in caves underneath nearby Alderley Edge.

When I went to prep school, I told my English master, Mr Day, that I was fed up with Enid Blyton and he told me to read Joan Aiken's *The Wolves of Willoughby Chase*, which I enjoyed. Mr Day drove to the school in his MG sports car and said that he found it almost impossible not to run over a sheep on the way, there were so many sheep. He was the first person I had ever met who didn't like sheep.

Not liking sheep is now almost a fashion, led by George Monbiot who, in his book *Feral*, describes landscapes that have been nibbled out of existence as 'sheep-wrecked'. A sheep is a non-native ruminant.

We always had a well-stocked library at home. And we were fascinated by a three-volume medical encyclopaedia called *The Science of Life*, co-authored by H.G. Wells, which came down through my mother's father, who had been an ear, nose and throat consultant.

My sister and I pored over some of the more macabre and grotesque illustrations of foetuses in bell jars and infants suffering from various degrees of cretinism. There was one startling photograph of a newborn baby in nappies, dangling from a stick being held by a white-coated lab assistant to demonstrate the prehensile ape skills of babies.

One picture showed a woman sweeping a floor again and again. It seemed that she had been sweeping the floor when she was interrupted to be told that her husband had died in the war. Consequently she could never stop sweeping. The condition was diagnosed as *dementia praecox* and so if, for example, in later life my sister would ask me to grate some cheese, I would always carry on grating until I had grated far too much so she would snatch the grater from me saying, 'Don't say you've got *dementia praecox*!'

Even when my sister is not around I persist in grating too much cheese for old times' sake.

Mother

MARY:

My mother was proud of her vegetable garden where she grew leeks, onions, potatoes, broad beans, green beans, peas, lettuce, tomatoes, raspberries and strawberries. She was particularly proud because of the money she was saving by growing things herself. Whenever I came back from London in winter she would boast that 'the freezer is coming down with raspberries', and it was poignant that she had not taken in that out-of-season raspberries (obviously not nearly so high in quality) were available in most English supermarkets.

The garden brimmed with potatoes of the very floury Irish variety called Queen which, when boiled in the steel saucepans of yore, would shed layer after pleasing layer of skins.

Every Saturday morning the butcher's van would drive up to the funeral yard, which abutted our kitchen window, and hand through a joint, like a giant chop, wrapped in greaseproof paper, complete with a hand-printed bill bearing the legend SMILEY GEORGE MASTER BUTCHERS OF LARNE.

Smiley George was not even a 'poncy' butcher. Properly hung meat, from animals who had lived happy lives before heading to the abattoir about a mile from our house, was available to all in those days and Smiley did not charge fancy prices or my mother would not have patronised him. Roast beef on Sunday was followed by mince/rissoles or cottage pie so at least 16 people were fed well out of something that cost the equivalent of £20 in today's money.

On Fridays a haunting cry would ring out through the town as a salesman went from street to street, URUNGU-RUNGURUNGURUNG ... but for some reason our mother did not buy herrings from him.

Giles's mother had been to Winkfield Place, Berkshire, where Constance Spry taught cordon bleu and flower arranging, and learned to cook properly, but convenience foods had just become available in England and so while his family was eating things like Shippam's paste and drinking Nesquik, my family was being well nourished.

We had chops occasionally and we had very good soup each day for lunch. My mother made the stock using most of a cooked chicken rather than just the bones and she threw in lots of other leftovers. 'You know, I just threw it together.' Today it would be called bone broth and sold at £9 per 600ml.

Then she was famed for her meringues, meringue flans, cherry chews, Jap cakes and flapjacks. Everyone in Ireland ate wheaten or soda bread with home-made jam or marmalade.

Giles has always been a very competitive cook. David, an art student and Giles's best friend from school, who was penniless, had realised that the way to a girl's heart was through her stomach and he more than compensated for being unable to afford to take girls to restaurants. Giles taught himself to cook when he first bought his tiny cottage, which we nicknamed Shortleat (as opposed to Longleat) because of its inadequacy, and he soon showed a flair for it.

Once Giles queried a dish that my mother had made. 'Can you tell me exactly how you made this kedgeree?' he asked in disapproving tones. The result of this veiled criticism was that the next time Betty invited me to come to the Province during the children's school holidays, she asked, 'Would you just bring the girls and not Giles? We're too old for him.'

Giles chuckled with delight when he heard he had been banned. He has always loved to think that he has 'made an impact' on another person, and that the thought of him has been preoccupying them.

About a year after the exclusion my mother asked, 'Well, would the four of you like to come for Easter?'

'But what about Giles?' I asked. 'I thought he was banned.'

'Ah,' she replied. 'I've granted him a fool's pardon.'

I loved every cell of my mother's body and everything about her – even her impatience and her other, very few, faults. And also her simplicity and lack of neurosis, her ability to enjoy life and think that her own life in this provincial town was absolutely marvellous. And the way she stood up to the bullies.

Once, in 1986, when my father was as usual lying in bed in the sitting room (she nursed him there for eight years after his stroke), there was a knock at 10pm on the glass door of our porch.

Betty went out and saw two masked men standing outside the porch. 'I opened the door and I said, "What do you want?" And they took off the masks and they said, "Oh sure, you don't recognise us." It was two of the policemen that Tim used to work with.' (My GP father had an extra role dubbed 'police surgeon', which meant he took samples from suspects and examined people before and after they were interrogated by the police to check they had not been beaten up. But before the Troubles he was mainly required to take blood or urine samples from drunks.)

'They said, "We've just been having a wee Christmas party in the station and we were missing the company of the doctor and we thought we'd call in on him and say hello." And I said, "Would you not have rung up if you were planning to call? He's fast asleep now." They said they were sorry and they went away.'

I said, 'Were you not frightened when masked men came to the door late at night? Why didn't you run upstairs and call the police?'

'Ah!' she said. 'I'd rather be dead than live in fear.'

Childhood Tape Recordings

GILES:

When we got our first cassette recorders, in those days made by either Bush or Philips, they seemed like a miracle because we now had the ability to tape our voices and make mock interviews, and we used to love to pretend to be doctors and patients with psychiatric problems.

Mental health fascinated us, perhaps because we had a schizophrenic uncle we had never met, a six-foot-five-inched, talented athlete and scholar to whom something – suspected to be a bullying incident – had happened during his National Service, and triggered some latent psychosis.

My father was consequently terrified of mental health issues and one of the manifestations of his terror was that as soon as anything weird, or anything that started to mess with his rigid sense of reality, for example the Beatles' *Magical Mystery Tour*, came on the TV, it was immediately switched off with all the determination of a latter-day Putin. This caused us to have a lifelong fascination with 'unsuitable' television, although this interest is wearing thin now as it seems there is *nothing but* weirdness on modern TV.

These predictable acts of sabotage made us dread him coming into the room when we were watching TV. There was no democracy in the family. Once the TV was off we would not dream of arguing with him because my mother, one of the last of the pre-feminist *Mad Men* era, used to say, 'You can only push a man so far.' I remember the sense of a miscarriage of justice.

Nevertheless, while our father was out, my sister and I would play a variation of Doctors and Nurses, and take it in turns to pretend to be either the doctor going around the psychiatric wards or one of the patients suffering from some sort of as yet unidentified syndrome. All this was as a result of reading these adult medical books which fired our imaginations. It was only a few years later that my sister and I watched what for us was one of the most thrilling childhood films, which was Elizabeth Taylor and Katharine Hepburn starring in *Suddenly, Last Summer*. This was truly grist to our mill.

Within the first opening shots we had Elizabeth Taylor in an asylum and my sister had a huge crush on Montgomery Clift. It made a welcome change from the boring films that we usually watched about Elvis in the army or Norman Wisdom films. All this interest in unsuitable films caused me to force my little brother, then aged nine, to watch *Quatermass and the Pit*, which he claims to this day damaged him as he was so frightened by it.

What parents don't think through today is that when their child goes for a sleepover with what seems like a wholesome family, there is nothing to stop older siblings from showing them stuff that is way beyond their age group, as was 'The Pit and the Pendulum' by Edgar Allan Poe. I would regard our sense of humour as 'Northern Gothic' in character.

Apart from recording our 'Doctor and Patients' sessions, one of the things I tried to do very early on with this recorder was to tape the plaintive cries, the loud, shrill 'pee-wit' of the flocks of peewits in the giant ash tree. They had a way of flying over the landscape that resembled synchronised swimmers. They seemed to merge into a super organism and they looked particularly impressive when flying over ploughed fields in winter and bobbing like a wave motion over the brown earth, contrasting the colour of the earth with their flapping wings and the flashes of their white flanks.

So I tried to tape them but I was unable to overcome the technical difficulties of not recording the wind as well so all I heard was the sound of the wind rushing into the microphone.

Peewits, also known as lapwings, were common farmland birds in the sixties. Last summer, I suddenly heard this evocative noise which sent me reeling back to the villa at Keele. A flock of up to 50 lapwings, which I hadn't heard since my childhood, above a large local field which, unusually, had been overlooked for a season and had escaped being managed to within an inch of its life.

It must have reminded the peewits of what the landscape might have looked like in the sixties – before the general use of broad-spectrum herbicides reduced fields to dead zones.

They behave in the most erratic way, sometimes plunging down like kamikaze pilots from a great height and giving off the piercingly squeaky noise that you hear when puppies are enjoying biting into a toy, but multiplied by 50. It is an attention-seeking cry that is impossible for a countryman to ignore; a melancholy cry redolent of moorland and wild places, and it connects you to tundra and the wild within you. This mysterious flock had suddenly appeared like a trace memory, a reminder of what the countryside could be if we could only make farming wildlife-friendly again.

The sort of countryside that most country dwellers want is not a monoculture. In the past there was not such a division between agricultural land and 'the countryside'. Now the two are almost entirely divorced. The tell-tale tramlines of crop sprayers mean your children will be inhaling deadly cocktails of pesticides at a time when their immune systems are not fully operational.

FLAT-SHARING IN LONDON

Section 2

THE MOVE TO THE COUNTRY

On why we upped sticks to
Wiltshire to start a country life

Why I Moved by Giles

GILES:

I spent some of a rainy afternoon last week at home in Wiltshire watching *Escape to the Country* during which I learned that Herefordshire was being branded as the 'New Cotswolds'. The 'Old Cotswolds' already cover a huge area – almost 800 square miles and running through five counties: Gloucestershire, Oxfordshire, Warwickshire, Wiltshire and Worcestershire. Isn't that big enough for people?

But it emerged that, since Covid, many folk from the south-east, including the beleaguered county of Kent (once described as 'now more of a lorry park or latrine than the Garden of England'), have settled in Herefordshire where they enjoy (for the time being) a quiet rustic life. The programme featured another couple looking to relocate into the 'real' Cotswolds and the presenter was quick to warn the 'openly same sex' couple that prices in Oxfordshire were 'way above the national average'.

I myself once lived in the Cotswolds. I spent a year there as a lodger in the mellow stone house of a divorced Scottish aristocrat. It was too quiet for a young man in his prime. But I had recently returned from a six-month stint in Ravenna, Italy, where I had become a fully trained

Byzantine mosaicist (having learned no money-making skills during my Fine Art course at Wimbledon College of Art). These were the starter days of my relationship with Mary, but I had no other interest in London life.

Consequently, I set up a studio (at a peppercorn rent) in a freezing barn owned by the aristocrat who was a friend's mother in the village of Adlestrop, only to find that there wasn't much call for Byzantine mosaics in the Cotswolds at the time. Now, of course, it is quite different – the place is saturated with City money – and I would have been quids in.

Either there was no call for it, or I gave such a negative account of myself – reverse marketing, as Mary described it (in fact urging those I met not to commission one of my mosaic panels) – that I look back on my year in the Cotswolds as yet another lost opportunity. One of those misunderstandings that seem to define my chequered career.

In fact, I spent the whole year on a single commission, but progress was slow. I was hampered by the knowledge that my client had bad taste and, since mosaic-making in itself is exacting and physically demanding work, it was even more difficult to create an image that I myself didn't like.

All around me was picture-perfect mellow dry stone, but I was desperately lonely there. Social life revolved around my divorced host's own social life. Every excuse to go to London was taken and there I was always given a warm welcome by the Kensington landlady where my future wife, Mary, had settled in an attic, following her own migration from parochial Northern Ireland.

After a year, news came through that my great uncle Tom had left me £24,000 in his will, and my mother and I headed straight to Essex where a close friend, Cyril, had bought a cottage. We found one for me in – as Mary grumbled – the only un-picturesque village in the whole area, but the price was right and it was only three miles from our friend, Cyril.

There I stayed for six years, gardening a manageably sized plot. It became obvious that this three up, three down period cottage in the middle of a terrace would not be big enough for Mary and our newborn baby, and somewhere else would have to be found. I miss Essex still, but Mary's social ambition was the driving factor that brought us to Wiltshire in 1988.

Why I Moved by Mary

MARY:

I left Northern Ireland and came to London for the noise and the people. I adored crowds and being jostled on the Tube. The thought of being in a place where, in almost every street, there was a pub or restaurant with lights on and people talking and laughing inside ... I wanted this. It wasn't the alcohol I wanted but the fact that there were people up and about.

I knew my home town in the Province contained the nicest people in the world – however, they were all *inside* for at least six nights of the week. It was dour socially in winter and even in summer, unless you were sporty; there was nowhere much to go except to congregate around the telephone box or head for the Regal cinema at 9.30pm. 'Let's go and watch the Regal getting out.'

By contrast, London was a non-stop party. However, I was lonely for the first two and a half years, until I found a social springboard by becoming a lodger in the house of an established Chelsea family. But even when lonely, there wasn't the same dankness and mournfulness as there had been at home because other people around you were having fun. You could always walk around a museum or Harrods and bask in the ambience of other people – even if you didn't know any of them. Looking back, I suppose other people were probably having cosy times inside their houses in Northern Ireland – as we are in this village now – but I wanted to see more action outside.

I never tired of London – although gradually I began to see, when I took up with Giles, that it was nice to go to the country at weekends and actually you weren't missing out on that much because most people we would have socialised with, in Giles's network, had also gone to the country at weekends.

Finally, my social life took off and I knew almost more people than I could process – even when socialising four nights a week. I was working on *Tatler* from 1984 to 1988, at the best moment in its history.

Why did young journalists want to be on *Tatler* in the eighties? My older friend Anne put it succinctly: 'In the sixties, it was pop stars; in the seventies, it was photographers; in the eighties, it's the upper classes. They are where it's at!'

The advent of Princess Diana in 1981 meant the popular perception of the upper classes changed. No longer were they seen as red-faced *The League of Gentlemen*-style, blood-sports-obsessed, blithering idiots. Now everyone wanted to know more about Diana's world and the focus shifted on to the tall and beautiful aristocrats like her.

Featuring Di on the cover, the 1982 number-one bestselling book in all categories was *The Official Sloane Ranger Handbook*. The whole country had become secretly interested in dovecotes, Barbours, wellies, Labradors, lawn meets, follies, polo, hunting, deb's delights, after-dinner games, house parties, estate agents, nannies in uniform and food throwing.

And *Tatler* was the only magazine covering them.

Those were the days when journalists were allowed lavish expenses and, all in the line of duty, we went out to breakfast, lunch, drinks and dinner with 'informants' – much of it subsidised by Condé Nast. We laughed almost continuously. The access and the voyeurism were glorious. We also laughed in the Beaufort Street maisonette we shared with Cyril, a writer and Mosh, then an artist and a wild dog Sam from Battersea Dogs Home. In the 1980s, Chelsea was still an artists quarter and friends came round every night at drinks time and gave me material to put into articles while Giles was constantly ready with Polyfilla to repair the jerry-built plasterwork.

I wouldn't have dreamed of moving away from all the fun. But, in 1988, our shared maisonette in Beaufort Street, Chelsea, came to an end when its owner Mosh moved to Barcelona. We couldn't live full-time in Essex as it was two and a half hours to London and I had only just got my foot in the door as a journalist. Therefore, we would have to sell Giles's cottage and move to London.

It was dispiriting looking at what was available. In those days it was £100,000 for a five-roomed conversion 'betwixt the railways' in Battersea. Yet there *was* a commutable village I knew about ...

Tatler's gardening and architectural expert, Candida Lycett Green, had told me the year before that she and her husband had bought the manor house of the 'best village in England'.

'It's a cul-de-sac at the foot of the downs,' she had told me. 'You can ride for miles without seeing anyone. It's 59 minutes to Paddington via the station three miles away, but best of all – it's a proper village without weekenders.'

One day, in *Tatler*'s fourth-floor office in Vogue House, while queueing for a bottle of Perrier in the days before coffee had become a thing, I had a closer look at a notice on the office corkboard. It had been up for weeks and was advertising a thatched hovel for £100,000. I had seen it before and had been vaguely wondering why such a dump would command such a high price when, that Friday afternoon, I suddenly noticed the magic name – *Candida Lycett Green Extension 2614*. I immediately unpinned the notice and went back to my desk. Candida was sitting opposite me on that day, tapping out on a manual typewriter an article about a garden in Cornwall belonging to some grandees in her network.

'Is this cottage in the village you were telling me about last year?' I showed her the page.

'Yes, and it's the nicest cottage in the whole of England and yet we haven't even had one viewing.'

'Giles and I will buy it,' I said there and then.

What had previously inhibited me from buying a cottage in a random village where we knew no one was the possibility that, even though it might look beautiful, we couldn't know that there wouldn't be hidden problems – overhead aerial training by fighter pilots, a sewage works, proposed developments of a sprawling housing estate.

I knew how beady Candida was and that, if she thought it was the nicest village in England to the extent that she had actually moved into it, then that was all the information I needed. Yes, she was selling a thatched hovel at the end of a terrace but the social opportunities of living in a satellite position to a manor house containing one of the most popular and well-connected women in the country meant I must seize this opportunity. I would have the best of both worlds.

'Well, that would be too good to be true if you bought it,' said Candida. 'Why not come to lunch tomorrow and see it?'

Giles and I drove down the next morning and as we turned off the A road and on to the one-mile track to the cul-de-sac village, we viewed the beauty of the bosomy and protective downs. At the entrance to the village stood an impressive Georgian rectory and beyond it a short street lined with a terrace of thatched cottages, one of which might be ours. As we turned up the lane to the church and the Manor Farm, before even looking at our potential new home, we decided we would buy it.

Part Two

Despatches from Wiltshire

'WHY HAVE THEY CHANGED JIF TO CIF, MARY?'

Section 3

COUNTRY SHOPPING ADVENTURES

On different approaches to shopping,
shop wars and the relocated Sloanes

GILES:

The word 'parochial' has negative connotations — suggesting blinkered insularity and a social drawbridge slammed shut for fear of the outsider. But the truth is that the parish itself, as Richard Mabey has noted, is a

'very laden concept. It has to do not just with geography and ecclesiastical administration, but with history and a system of loyalties. For most of us, it is the indefinable territory to which we feel we belong, of which we have the measure. Its boundaries are more the limits of our intimate allegiances than lines on a map. These allegiances have always embraced wild life as well as human...

I am not sure if it is possible to feel these allegiances after one has moved out of a childhood landscape where we, for example, were known as a 'Potteries family' and where Mary was a member of a long-established 'medical family' and into a completely new one whose residents share no history. Correction, I think it is possible, but probably only after a generation. People move around these days, following their jobs, or in my case following Mary's social ambitions, so how can we feel the true sense of belonging enjoyed by the indigenae. Mary likes it, though even she feels deracinated.

GILES:

It is a truth universally acknowledged that men don't like shopping and women do. In Mary's case she seems to confuse shopping with achievement.

I have given her the moniker 'Bad Buy Killen', which upsets her, but all through our marriage Mary has consistently returned in triumph, from trips to the nearby town, bearing purchases that turn out to be bad buys.

On one occasion, when we were packing for Christmas with some friends in Worcestershire, we found her wrapping, as presents, three hideous carrier bags made of hessian. She swore these were designer bags made by Lulu Guinness and was disconcerted by our heartless laughter.

There was the washing-up bowl with a hole in its base for 'swifter drainage', and one night I became aware of low-level whirring noises, which I could not identify and thought might be presaging a mini-stroke.

We have an insectocutor-style LED electric fire in front of which our Tibetan spaniel, Merlin, likes to bask, especially when it is in rotate mode. I moved quickly to turn this off, thinking it might be about to explode, but the noise persisted. It was then that my eyes alighted on a cheap plastic clock, proudly displayed on the mantlepiece, its charity-shop price sticker bearing the legend '£7.50'.

To me £7.50 could have bought us a free-range chicken so I resented the purchase – and more so when I found that the clock itself was the source of the noise. The minute hand was racing around the clock face like something out of the film *Back to the Future* and showed no sign of stopping. It was one of the most surreal things I have ever seen. And so I raced upstairs to show Mary this supernatural phenomenon. Unfortunately she was asleep, so I was forced to remove the battery to put a stop to the nuisance before she had even witnessed it. Then I realised this nuisance was the precise reason why the previous owner had donated it to the charity shop.

MARY:

It was annoying to me that Giles was so quick to dismiss this clock as a bad buy and insist on returning it to the charity shop. Later, it turned out that the reason the hands had been racing around the face of their own accord was that it was the sort of clock that needs to be paired by Bluetooth with Alexa, so you could use it as a way of timing yourself while doing chores. If he had only allowed me the opportunity to master the technology, with the help of a technology-literate junior assistant, it could have been very useful to us. Moreover, although plastic, it was rather elegant and a bargain at £7.50.

GILES:

What I call a bargain is something which costs £2 or £3 but Mary's idea of a bargain is something which can cost £8, £13 or even £17.50. These items contribute daily to the unwinnable war against clutter in the cottage where – to use an analogy from nature – it has reached the high tide mark.

I try to avoid shopping myself. I never have shopped in London – except in the days when we lived in Beaufort Street, Chelsea, in the eighties when I would reluctantly patronise Europa, the local late-night 'rip-off' grocery store when it was my turn to cook supper for the four inmates – Mary, myself, Cyril and Mosh.

I remember feeling bitter at having to spend about 20 per cent more than I needed to have done for the sort of staple ingredients that I used to cook with in those days, namely mince, onions, garlic, tinned tomatoes, spaghetti and Cheddar cheese. Or the ingredients for kedgeree or Coronation chicken or chilli con carne. But, as Mary never failed to remind me, there was nothing to stop me from going to the Sainsbury's on the King's Road earlier in the day – except my lack of ability to think ahead.

MARY:

There was another mismanagement factor that put up the cost of living in the Beaufort Street flat. We didn't have a dishwasher or a rota about 'turns' for washing up. This meant that on at least three nights a week (we went away every weekend) we couldn't eat in the flat at all because the sink was piled so high we couldn't access the tap. Consequently we had to go out to Wine & Kebab on the Fulham Road for chicken kebabs and rice with house wine, thus wasting a collective around £100 a week in today's money.

Two Styles of Shopping

GILES:

Here in Wiltshire the shops have been increasingly pon-cified with each passing year. The other day a depressing item in the property pages of the *Sunday Times* revealed that in the so-called 'race for space', 'virtually every rural property near the A303 has been picked off by London-ers wanting to relocate after Covid'.

But there is a notable difference between the shops serving the tastes of relocated Londoners and the long-established village shops, which seem to take pride in being neither pushy nor efficient. One example is our local bakery whose products are much sought-after by those in the know but is so un-pushy that unless you live in the village, you would not even know the premises existed behind its steamed-up windows and virtually invisible fascia.

I recently entered at 11.50am to buy two of their popular pasties for lunch. There were only two pasties in the glass display unit. The baker explained to me: 'You're lucky there's two left. They tend to all go early now. People who want pasties for their lunch know they have to come in early in the morning, otherwise they are all gone. And from about midday till about three we are turning away folk who want pasties. We have to say, "We have sold out. You need to come in earlier if you want them. Or you need to order them. If you order them, we will keep them for you."'

The oven is on the premises but it has clearly not occurred to the bakers to make more pasties to meet with demand. I once suggested, 'Why don't you make more and then, if you find you have made too many, offer them at half price around closing time?'

She explained that no they couldn't do that because 'if it got out that they would be sold at half price around closing time, everyone would wait until closing time and there would be a rush to buy at half price and no sales made during the day.'

MARY:

I was worried about the amount of unhealthy starch and fat Giles was eating per day, all sourced from this bakery – sausage rolls, croissants, doughnuts and traditional pasties – but short of asking the bakery to ban him as a customer, I have no way of stopping him going in there.

Instead, I bribed him to go for three weeks eating only healthy food for lunch. It was a financial bribe. The problem then was that Giles said he was too busy to cook lunch and I then had to prepare his lunch for him, which is of course time-consuming. One of the reasons Giles gets away with so much is that he does cook most of the food and he is good at cooking.

GILES:

In truth, the very act of simply noticing what is going down the gullet had an almost immediate beneficial effect with the loss of 12 pounds in three weeks. Now that their principal customer has deserted it, I worry about the fate of our local bakery, purveyors of Wiltshire's finest Cornish pasties, sausage rolls, doughnuts and another product whose main ingredient is the rendered fatty tissue of a pig – lardy cake.

The latter was not popular with me because I found the taste of lard too primitive for someone who had not been brought up in the county. Moreover, if you call someone a lardy cake in Wiltshire it is an insult.

The expectant faces of the hair-netted bakery counter girls, seeing me go past the window but not coming in, were too much to bear so I went in to explain.

'I'm on nettle soup now, I'm on an anti-inflammation diet,' I enunciated, channelling my best Kenneth Williams. 'According to my new bible, *Hedgerow Medicine* by Julie Bruton-Seal and Matt Seal, our ancestors here in the Vale of Pewsey used to find the vitamin C content of nettles provided a valuable spring tonic after a winter living on ancient and salted meat.'

But my attempt at affability was rebuffed.

MARY:

A nearby novelty store stocks a multiplicity of unexpected items – dog food and stationery for example, along with wicker baskets from Vietnam and not from the local withy beds. I wanted some see-through plastic boxes in which to store out-of-season clothes in the attic and was delighted, when entering, to see a row of differently sized lids stacked against a wall. I picked up the size I needed and walked to the counter.

'Can I have two boxes to match this size lid?'

'No, we don't have the boxes,' said the woman at the counter proudly. 'We only have the lids.'

I don't object. It makes a change from the experience of shopping in a city where personnel, trained in the psychology of shopping, wait like predators. They ask whether they can help you as soon as you walk in and the pressure to buy begins to build. I welcome the lack of hypocrisy and the disinterest evinced in country shops.

Even the charming café at the Garden Centre, where dogs are welcome and the staff make upmarket paninis, is closed, despite demand for a seven-days-a-week service, on three of them – and stops taking orders for hot food at 3pm.

GILES:

The absence of sycophancy in our traditional local shops reached its apogee in the much-missed D'Arcy's bookshop in Devizes. I had to do something to kill time as chauffeur to Mary, who had endless dental appointments in that town, and I used to do this in the glorious antiquarian bookshop, D'Arcy's – a unique resource for the idle, the curious or the man with a grasshopper mind in search of hidden knowledge on diverse subjects that for the sake of categorisation could be classified as 'against the grain' of conventional wisdom.

I would happily spend an hour in there browsing undisturbed. Mr D'Arcy himself, usually sitting at his roll-top desk in the 18th century building with a glass of red wine in front of him, would barely look up as I walked in – in a paradoxical form of politeness. He clearly didn't want to put his customers under any pressure to purchase by even acknowledging their presence. The only thing that interrupted the ticking of the grandfather clock was the pop of the cork.

An Unsightly Gilet

GILES:

I enjoy the occasional trip to Burbage, an unimproved village with a builder's merchant/country store. We went to pick up some wood preservative for our carpenter, who doesn't drive. I don't mean to imply he is our carpenter in a *Downton Abbey* way, just that, as an adherent of the philosophy of Slow Living, he has been building a shed for us for so many years that I now think of him as a permanent feature of cottage life and hence refer to him as 'our' carpenter. Patrick (the highly skilled master carpenter who served a seven-year apprenticeship) has hinted that we are very lucky to have him since all workmen he knows of have got work till the end of time, due to the fact that no one is moving house and everyone is improving the one they are currently living in.

While in Burbage I took the opportunity to pick up an unsightly sleeveless gilet of the type worn by the commendably honest ex-MP Neil Parish, who admitted watching porn when looking for a tractor brand named Dominator and falling into a rabbit hole of sin when he was redirected to a site called Dominatrix. I explained to Mary that I thought I would use the gilet to flag up my support for Parish as he seemed like a nice gentle chap, a hapless and genuinely harmless bumpkin, caught up in the tailwinds of the Tory sleaze hurricane.

I also had the satisfaction of returning a pair of gardening gloves I'd purchased there which I considered had worn out too quickly. I explained that I didn't want a refund, I just wanted them to stop stocking that particular brand. The shopkeeper was perfectly agreeable and said he would mention it to his boss.

MARY:

The gilet is an eyesore. Moreover, regarding the gloves, I thought his tone had been faintly accusatory when he returned them to the shopkeeper. It could well be the case that Giles himself had plunged the brown gloves into creosote and forgotten he'd done so. This might well have explained their rapid deterioration.

Buying New Glasses

MARY:

Giles likes the results of shopping, i.e. food on his table, but he dislikes the procedure of it. The idea that this is time 'wasted', i.e. which could be spent in the garden, torments him so much that he thinks the only way to shop is to be quick and decisive ... even when making key purchases such as glasses.

When he found out from our accountant that a new pair could be offset against tax as a necessary tool of trade, he agreed to let me make an appointment with the local optician. We made simultaneous appointments for the same day because I also needed new glasses.

I am fascinated by the optician. She looked 20 if not 30 years younger than she had looked the last time I saw her. She must be at least 50 as she has a son in his mid-thirties but she had grown her hair long and was wearing it in a ponytail, which really suits her. Her daughter-in-law works in Cambridge on epigenetics and we talked about this and other scientific topics on which I have theories. Perhaps I stayed in the cubicle ten minutes longer than was strictly necessary but, when I came out, Giles was already making a payment at the counter.

'I don't muck about,' he boasted, grinning at the receptionists. 'Unlike you, Mary, I don't need to spend the whole day over a simple purchase. To be quick and decisive is a political act. I represent a human bulwark against the tyranny of choice.'

I wasn't even allowed to see which frames he had selected. When we went to collect them a week later, however, we found that he had been *too* quick off the mark with his decisiveness.

The glasses are Ray-Bans and, though the shape suits him, there are two distracting silver studs dominating the edge of the frames. Worse, Ray-Ban is written in embossed, large letters on each spectacle arm.

'Oh,' said Giles, 'I hadn't noticed that. Why didn't you point that out to me, Mary? I don't want to be a walking advert for Ray-Ban. Is there any way I could rub these letters off with coarse sandpaper?' he asked the bewildered receptionists, who clearly thought that to be a walking advert for Ray-Ban would be a plus.

GILES:

Maybe only a very few people in Britain would consider it a minus to have Ray-Ban embossed on the arms of their glasses but I am one of them. In my day, wearing a brand name on a piece of clothing or equipment was considered 'a bit Charlie', a phrase which has gone out of fashion or, in today's parlance, a bit naff. Maybe even that expression has gone out of fashion ... 'vulgar' would be an even more old-fashioned term.

Giles's Variable Taste Disorder

MARY:

Nothing makes me happier than when a compliant friend with a driving licence takes me on a tour of the local charity shops. There are at least 11 in nearby Devizes. Yet all my exciting finds are invariably disparaged by Giles. 'We have enough clutter already,' he grumbles when I display them.

It's a different story when I have acquired a little luxury of the sort we have needed for years – for example a spare transistor radio for the bathroom – but only if I have stuck a sticker on to it saying, 'Shaw Ridge Charity Shop £2'. I always hold on to charity-shop stickers so I can reapply them to brand-new purchases when necessary.

He himself is subject to impulse buys – it all depends on how much coffee he has had of a morning. He once bought, from a market stall, a spring-loaded coin dispenser converted from a First World War cartridge shell and used it to dispense coins to part pay his Jungian psychoanalyst on Boars Hill, Oxford. He considered it a great achievement that he often managed to annoy the analyst while doing this.

To add to his existing condition of Variable Intelligence Disorder, he also suffers from Variable Taste Disorder. The first warning sign came with the purchase of a cushion from a charity shop at Brandon near Thetford. It was made of faux tapestry finish and bore the legend 'Lord of the Manor'. Giles placed it on the Parker Knoll chair in our television room and beamed proudly as he channelled Benny from the Crossroads Motel.

'Where did that come from?'

'I bought it.'

'But you never buy anything.'

'No, not before today, but it's beautiful and the price was right. It was ten pounds reduced from fifteen.'

The most offensive purchase he has made when caffeinated is a large, beige, plastic mopping bucket which I consider disfigures the whole downstairs of the cottage.

The second most offensive is a picnic blanket in vivid pink tartan, impregnated with sufficient chemicals to allow it to double as an insect repellent. Both were bought as a result of him having had too much coffee that morning.

My Joy in Shopping

MARY:

He's right that I see shopping as an achievement. To me it is one. Just as Giles feels a sense of achievement when he has planted a row of potatoes, I feel it is an achievement to arrive back from an expedition of hunter-gathering with a purchase I believe to be beautiful and know to be useful.

Perhaps due to early deprivation, I associate shopping with a sense of power and emotional fulfilment. When I was a child, children didn't have 'spending money'. We had pocket money and, similar to Giles, I used to save all mine up to buy, from the china shop in our provincial town, ceramic dogs and horses for my parents, which I now realised they couldn't have wanted. In those days it was me who was disfiguring the house with my purchases.

I once bought my mother a necklace made of multi-coloured plastic balls linked with the sort of metal chain that leaves a black stain against your neck. I insisted she wore it to a ball she was going to – and, because she was a decent sort and she had promised she would, she did so. No doubt it completely ruined her look.

Giles in Waitrose

GILES:

The Waitrose in Marlborough makes more profit per square foot than any other Waitrose in the country. Mary loves going there but I don't. The aspirational lifestyle aspect gets me down – and the phrase 'food pornography' always springs to mind as I comb the shelves looking, often in vain amongst the excess, for a product I know they stock but which has been moved, as is their exasperating habit, as if to indulge in some huge practical joke against their elderly customers. So much so that I now blurt out to the harmless school leavers who are stacking the shelves for work experience, 'Where have you hidden the Gentleman's Relish *this time*?'

On the credit side, Waitrose does stock very good fish. I am not yet ready, for ecological reasons, to give up fish on Fridays and sometimes it is marked down in price on that day. And I am willing to risk microdosing on mercury or plastics, which is one of the perils of eating any fish these days.

And they do have a good class of celebrity shopper. Jon Snow, the former Channel 4 anchorman, can be seen shopping there, Simon Russell Beale, Nigel Havers, David Hemery and David Owen of the Gang of Four, who agonised for so long about leaving the Labour Party and setting up the SDP with Shirley Williams. I sometimes find myself even looking out for Lady Isobel Barnett but Mary tells me she died years ago.

Giles in the Co-Op

GILES:

The Pewsey Co-op, the most unponcey local option, is, paradoxically, just as expensive as Waitrose. Morale in the Co-op is low – possibly because of the disgrace of their former chairman, the 'Crystal Methodist'; possibly because it is always too cold in there; and probably because a soundtrack of breaking local news is constantly droning at a low level in the background – and often these stories seem to be about paedophiles or rapists on the run.

I once took issue when I saw the DVD of *Hostel* sitting there in the 'impulse buy' section near the till. I told the assistant that I was sure the founding fathers of the Co-operative Society would have felt that the dissemination of 'torture porn' should not be perceived as part of the mission statement. The assistant said she would look into it and the next time I went in the DVD had been removed.

The only good thing that you could say about the Co-op is that it does have a photo booth. Otherwise you are paying the same prices as Waitrose while not having the same quality.

Giles in Lidl

GILES:

By contrast, I get the same sense of elation from entering Lidl as I do from shopping in a Carrefour hypermarket in France. I feel light-headed, as though I have just stepped off a Ryanair flight into Europe.

Lidl has the drawback of being 25 minutes' drive away from the cottage and, if you happen to forget to bring a £1 coin, it is almost impossible to do your shopping as you cannot manage without the trolleys. Waitrose, by contrast, seems to trust its customers not to make off with the trolleys.

Lidl also sells vegetable seeds in the spring. They are cheaper and more plentiful in the packet than those available in the garden centres. Everything about Lidl seems to me to raise two fingers to the rest of 'Rip-off Britain'.

It's the same story with vegetables, superb ready-to-eat avocados, ground coffee at half the price of other supermarkets, and Serrano ham impaled into a carving block made of wood (from 'sustainable plantations'). These hams are, of course, too big for the fridge but are great for anyone with a cold larder or outhouse where they can put a dome over one.

Their frozen fish includes white anchovies in seawater – delectable. None of their staples such as meat or canned tomatoes is lacking in flavour or quality. Sometimes they have themed sections – like a whole area devoted to Greek food.

We once found a local high-end professional caterer shopping at Lidl and virtually clearing the shelves of its supplies of sliced white bread. She looked guilty when she saw me and Mary but she told us she used the bread for the making of 'bridge sandwiches'. Her profit margins must have grown since switching to Lidl, which I see as the nemesis to Waitrose.

Incidentally it is possible to time your visits for best advantage – go at teatime, 5pm, when strivers are winding down at home putting their feet up.

The best garden shears I ever purchased were from Lidl. Yet even though I knew I would shortly need another pair, I failed to observe the Darwinian injunction above every shelf 'WHEN IT'S GONE IT'S GONE'. I didn't panic-buy and have never been able to coincide another visit to Lidl with the availability of that same brand of shears.

Moreover there is the 'Lidl in the Middle' central aisle to tempt the impulse shopper with a constantly changing range of offerings such as electric foot spas, design-classic stepladders at £34, and waterproof trousers for the whole family.

I had to be almost talked down from making an impulse buy of a two-seater kayak, made of reinforced PVC with its own patented inflator pump. I was instantly thinking of the fun that would be had by launching it on my brother's carp pond and the jolly time we could have with my nephews, paddling along some private trout stream in a bid to free the waterways while being shouted at by an irate landowner. There are hardly any rivers where you are allowed to go on a canoe or kayak because there are so many 'riparian rights'.

The only bad experience I have had with Lidl was when I purchased a kabanos Mediterranean sausage. To be fair, I was probably not supposed to eat it all at once. Afterwards I had to lie writhing in the foetal position on the floor of Room 4 for 20 minutes until Mary produced Gaviscon to relieve the symptoms.

I would more than happily serve as a brand ambassador. My catchphrase would be 'I'm Lidl Class'; however, realistically I would be reluctant to take on such a paid role as it would inevitably require me to tour the country and make appearances at the various branches. As a stay-at-home dad, this wouldn't suit me.

A Love of Vintage

MARY:

In the 1970s, when I went to stay with my English cousin, Michael, a vicar in Harrow, I used to take the Tube to Oxford Circus or Knightsbridge, holding an *A–Z*, and just wander around the shops, admiring the goods but not buying anything. I couldn't afford any of the things but I was simply entranced to see them anyway.

Liberty, with its exquisite panelled rooms and rolls of lawn cotton, its jewellery, its dresses costing 40 or 50 times what I could dream of spending on a dress myself, its elegant salesgirls and well-presented salesmen ... I could hardly believe that I was even allowed to enter Liberty, or indeed Harrods, and just marvel at the beauty of the goods, sometimes even being allowed to handle them.

But once I had met my flatmate Camilla, whom I joined as a lodger in her family house in Chelsea, I never lusted after first-hand clothing.

Camilla was stylish. She led me to the church jumble sale of St Mary's, near Sloane Square, to which local grandees had donated their cast-offs. There was no competition for these items in the 1970s because it was an age when almost every other girl slavishly adhered to the styles decreed to be in fashion that season. Moreover other girls perceived second-hand clothes as rather disgusting.

To be fair, second-hand pants and shoes *are* disgusting but not Dior dresses, Victorian camiknickers (gusset free) and hand-embroidered silk shawls.

Camilla would have seemed an eccentric figure had she not been so strikingly attractive and confident. Gradually she was copied. Including by me and her own mother. Camilla's father used to call his wife an 'Oxfemme fatale'.

Over the years, vintage has become mainstream. There are few bargains to be had in second-hand shops as these have usually already been spotted by the likes of Bay Garnett to be resold via Oxfam Vintage or by professional vintage clothes finders to be sold on eBay.

But fortunately there is no longer the pressure there once was to be 'in season' and I can re-wear my small wardrobe again and again, buy jumpers from the online site Nearly New Cashmere and intercept my multi-millionaire friends as they are heading to the charity shops with carloads. Meanwhile I can posture that it is for ethical reasons that I have stopped shopping for clothes – which is not a lie.

Over-Caffeinated at the Garden Centre

GILES:

There was a time when garden centres were just that, but they have come a long way since Percy Thrower's day. Today they suffer from mission creep, to borrow military terminology. Now you are just as likely to find hardware, stationery, camping equipment, kitchenware, statuary, aisles of figurines and enough cushions to fill a quarry. And even books. I recently found myself browsing a volume by a Mr Gordon Kerr titled *Houses of Death – Horrific Secrets Behind Closed Doors*. Fascinating though it was, the connection to horticulture remained elusive.

On a recent mercy dash to North Wales to look after my elderly mother, who lives in a prime beauty spot overlooking the Menai Strait and Snowdonia, she asked me to fetch her some firelighters and I suggested that I drive down to the nearest garden centre, which would be sure to stock them. I set off with her words ringing in my ears: 'Darling, you would need a whole morning to see it all.'

Sure enough, some hours later, I emerged, having left no solar-powered pebble unturned. I was ineluctably drawn from one aisle to the next, like a Bedouin lost in a souk. Well, with ample free parking, working customer toilets and a café boasting 'Mains at £6.99 per portion' it was easy to see why it was heaving with time-wasters like myself on a Monday morning.

Only the night before, I had been reading George Monbiot's *Feral*, in which the author postulates that the popularity of shopping dates back to the days when we would return to our caves in triumph bearing hunted or gathered 'stuff'. In those days, that stuff was for our survival; today, it is for our vain pleasure.

Hence I allowed myself to be drawn further and further into the aisles as I explored the goods on offer to see if there was any resonance with my own inner hunter-gatherer.

I spent 15 minutes examining a rack of novelty walking sticks. I thought I might buy one for Mary, to pre-empt falls. I also fancied a blue 'height-adjustable' tartan shooting stick, in case we shrink, as we are unlikely at this stage of life to grow in stature. For myself, a cane with a number 8 pool ball handle, which was surprisingly difficult to grip. It reminded me of Reginald Perrin's cowrie ashtrays – which were full of holes. A battery-powered Kentish lantern, made in China, caught my eye, as did an 'Aphrodite's Cascade' hand-painted with a granite ceramic finish; it was solar-powered, which, in full sunlight, meant it would produce a gentle trickle of water, reminiscent of an elderly gentleman peeing.

By now, I needed a rest and was drawn to one of four giant upturned hands made of tropical hardwood. I sat down just in time to spot a 'please do not sit on the chair's' [sic] notice' designed to deter loiterers like myself. Philosophy students at Oxford spend whole terms debating the meaning of a chair that you can't sit on but I didn't have time to ponder that question.

I was being irresistibly drawn to two life-sized budgerigars on perches of yellow poly resin. They were £5.49 apiece. Nice at each end of the cottage mantlepiece, I thought. But I confess I was falling more for a three-quarter-life-sized Labrador of exquisite workmanship and also in poly resin which, for £69, seemed like a bargain when you factor in ten years' worth of no vets bills, kibble or Cesar pouches.

Four hours later, I related my experiences of the garden centre to my mother as I lit the woodburner. 'If you *had* bought it, darling, I would have had no hesitation in contacting a local mental health professional,' she trilled.

Sloaney Shops and Foodie Destinations

MARY:

Last year we discovered that a farm shop had opened up on a local farm and I went there with Gug, who has bought a cottage in Stanton St Bernard a few miles away as Giles was too 'busy' in the garden to drive me there.

Gug was delighted to find within this shop a plethora of Food without Chemicals. Focaccia, all cuts of pork from the farmer's free-range pigs, new potatoes covered with soil, handmade spelt biscuits and ice cream from milk from their own herd, box after box of green and red vegetables.

Gug has attracted a sophisticated wife who is used to visiting friends at all points of the globe and eating rarefied cuisine. 'Oh my God,' enthused Gug when he saw the range on offer. 'Amber will go mad when she sees this shop. It will make her want to stay in the Pewsey Vale rather than moving to Ludlow.'

'But Ludlow is a backwater,' I replied. 'Why would she want to move there?'

'Well, it's become a foodie destination,' said Gug before reeling off the names of a gang of 'cool' people who have bought houses in satellite dwellings to a local foodie's big house. As with our own purchase. Satellite Dwelling Syndrome is an overlooked factor in the relocator's agenda. There should be a book about it.

He and I bought some handmade sausage rolls and sat in his car eating them as we took in the glorious local landscape with nothing of ugliness as far as the eye could see. That night we ate free-range pork chops made from the farmer's free-range pigs. The taste, compared to the standard-issue pork chop from a supermarket, was incomparable. They were accompanied by a variety of black potatoes, black not just on the outside but also on the inside and highly flavoursome. The only thing that spoiled the occasion was Giles grumbling that he bet the shop had seen us coming.

Another time, I received a friendly email from the Manor Farm reminding me about the plant sale in their barn. It was so friendly that I was incentivised to go because I'm never sure if people have gone off me or not.

I brought with me Elouise, a friend of our daughter Fleur. Patrick the carpenter was laying a new floor in Fleur's bedroom and Elouise, who had come to stay for a mini break, was sleeping along with Fleur in our younger daughter Rosie's bedroom, one in a single bed, one in a double, side by side, as though they were two little girls.

At 11.20 I said I would set off for the Manor Farm without Elouise unless she was ready and so she came with me. As we arrived at the barn behind the Manor Farm, where they were selling plants and cakes, I found I only had a £10 note. No one has cash any more because you so rarely need it except for the occasional parking meter that is non digital.

It was £3 to get in. I bought a cake at £3.50 and then a courgette plant and some lemon verbena to make herbal tea from its leaves. Elouise, who makes £1,000 per week working from home at a really boring job getting 'permissions' – something to do with the film world – bought another £15 worth.

I chatted to the thatcher and about five other people. A tour of the Manor Farm garden was also thrown in and I wandered around with the others. It was a fun place to make small talk. As I never tire of noting, walking and talking is the tool of truth. Lots of stuff emerges while neighbours are looking ahead rather than into one another's eyes. I explained that Giles was too busy working in his own garden to make an appearance at the well-ordered Manor Farm. Another villager riposted that she would love to know what Giles does in his garden all day but 'none of us can see because of all the bushes'.

The Sloane Ranger still exists but she has been driven out of Chelsea by excessive prices. How funny to think that in the 1950s and 1960s Chelsea was regarded as a slum by grandees who, in those days, favoured Belgravia or Knightsbridge.

But, as has been historically observed, where artists congregate, property inflation follows. Chelsea is now home to bankers and oligarchs and the very foundations of the houses have been undermined by drilling and excavations necessary to allow private swimming pools and gyms to be installed for the security-conscious occupants.

The late Julian Barrow, president of the Chelsea Art Society, could often be seen shopping at Green & Stone, Chelsea's oldest art store, established 1927. Despite it being so pricey, Julian used to say that if even he couldn't shop for art materials in Chelsea, it would sound the death knell of this former artists' quarter. James Whistler and John Singer Sargent had both painted in Julian's Tite Street studio.

However the Green & Stone landlords rented the flats above to high net worth individuals. Apparently, the resulting installation of power showers meant that the Victorian plumbing could not cope and the shop was flooded with sewage five times in two months. Eventually even Green & Stone, one of the most magical shops in Chelsea, who had supplied material to Francis Bacon, Prince Philip and Edward Seago, had to move out and make way for the inevitable. The store has relocated a mile down the road, and taken its artistic community with it.

Here in Wiltshire, the Sloane, by which I mean a public-school-educated rural relocator, makes an annual appearance at a Christmas sale where goods such as handmade pyjamas, muslin washrags and hair ornaments are sold at upmarket prices to buyers whose names have been harvested from well-connected address-book owners. It's cheering when the seasonal invitations come in, but then awkward when you enter the converted barn where these sales typically now take place. (Time was when the relocating Sloane set her heart on an old rectory. Today's younger version wants a converted barn.) This is because, on entry, you are enthusiastically greeted by people selling things they have either made or 'sourced' themselves, invariably things in perfectly good taste but often things you don't actually want. However, in general the Sloane input to the world of country shopping is benign.

Our friend Gug's village has an honesty cupboard set into the wall near the centre. From it you can buy milk, cream, apple juice and vegetables, and just put the cash into the nominated box belonging to the relevant supplier. Stanton, whose ethos is led by Sloanes, has evolved into an Ealing Comedy-type of village, where everyone makes an effort to help each other. Sir Richard Paget comes and collects all the fallen apples and pears, and squashes them into juice, gives a certain percentage back to the householder, selling the rest at local foodie shops.

Class Wars and the Village Shop

MARY:

Sloanes are fine running their own shops with members of their own tribes, but problems can arise when a Sloane is appointed in a superior position to a long-standing local worker.

There can be taste wars when the Sloane is appointed to run an existing rural shop or business and the local long-term worker, in a subordinate position, is made to feel small when a new clientele with money to spend swarms into the business to buy unfamiliar, sophisticated goods or foods made by artisans.

'They see them coming,' remarked one of our neighbours regarding such a shop.

'Yeah and they see them going again too – I wouldn't shop there, 'retorted her interlocutor.

Louise, a benevolent local landowner who, for some reason, enjoys coming to our cottage and washing up as well as taking me, a non-driver, 'motoring' in her comfortable car, recently picked me up and we drove 20 minutes together to a village near Devizes to visit Jenny, a seamstress, who can do proper sewing and mending and does it in a repurposed tool shed at the end of her minuscule garden, working happily away with the doors open and her husband strimming and tidying up their garden, which features rock pools whose fish contents had just been raided by a passing heron.

Louise knew Jenny was good but had stopped using her when she moved away from Louise's village to one near mine. Propinquity had prompted Louise to use a new seamstress who had pushed a card through her letter box saying she had relocated from London where she had a mending and sewing business, and Louise decided to give her a chance. But the new seamstress had charged £900 for making ten cushions with washcovers for outdoor furniture – these featured cheap nylon zips and shrank in the wash.

By contrast old country seamstress Jenny was still producing traditional good quality work out of her repurposed tool shed. Jenny was not impressed by the foam that the relocator had used and showed Louise a better quality, firmer foam that might be used for the replacement cushions. At a cost of only £35 for a full lounger mattress base, Louise quickly realised how much she had overpaid for the shoddier goods with their fancy London prices.

Relocated Sloanes are not all seen, by indigenae, as interfering or incompetent newcomers who disturb the status quo. They often help to run the village shop in those villages lucky enough to have one. The one in nearby Shalbourne, which makes only a tiny profit, is run by a committee of community-spirited volunteers and, as it is the only shop in the village of 400 people, it is literally a lifeline. Who needs a Harrods Food Hall-style emporium of products if you can purchase just the basics by walking a few yards along the road?

Why does not the government, if it seriously wishes to reduce emissions and promote mental health, introduce subsidies for village shops? Those Shalbourne residents who do not use the shop say it is because, for example, teabags are 20 pence more expensive there than they are in Waitrose in Marlborough.

I suggest a law compelling each Waitrose or Aldi – or whatever the dominant supermarket in the nearest big town is – to supply to the village shop the essential items such as teabags, coffee, dog food, bread and eggs at the same price as they are in the big branch in town. The price matching would certainly be the swing factor which could persuade villagers to just stroll along to the shop and get a bit of exercise while so doing, rather than getting into their cars. Forty lots of emissions per day are calculated to have not been emitted in the village of Shalbourne because the car owner saw no need to drive to the town when they could buy the basics at the village shop.

The elderly would be able to have one conversation a day, which would be enough to keep the isolated feeling human and the fragile under observation. Moreover, in a Miss Marple way, the casual exchange of gossip is invaluable – for example:

'I'm sure I saw some young men with hoods on trying the gate to the Old Rectory last night. I stopped to ask if I could help them but they said they were looking for a lost dog.'

'Oh yes. Christine saw them too. The cameras in her barn picked them up nosing about there in the middle of the night.'

Result: two and two are put together and security footage of the hooded youths appears in the local paper. If they are not identified, they still think twice about trying it on in that village again. These days the local *Gazette & Herald* runs a gratifying section listing the activities of the court of Petty Sessions. Names of culprits and their punishments are printed. It must be a disincentive.

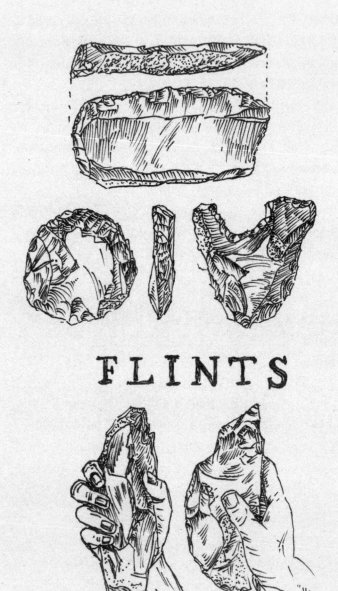

A SELECTION OF WORKED FLINT IMPLEMENTS

Section 4

TOWN VERSUS COUNTRY

On the perils of the 'race for space',
finding wildness on a Cotswolds mini
break and the joy of looking down

MARY:

It is often asked why did it take the pandemic for it to dawn on people that it is much nicer to live in the country and that you can get more bang for your buck?

They forget what life was like before you could send in your work electronically and before 'long-distance telephone calls' became affordable.

Moreover, the original point of the cities was that they were cultural hubs. Time was when all interesting and talented young creatives would head for London to be where the action was. But once it became impossible to find anywhere affordable to live in London, the artists and creatives had no choice but to move out – currently they are colonising the south coast, the area around Bruton in Somerset and Faversham in Kent.

So now there are multiple smaller cultural hubs around the country, you don't have to travel so far to meet like-minded people. Time was when country dwellers had to accept that the trade-off for the space and beauty would be social starvation.

In 1928 the writer Evelyn Waugh was staying with the Sitwells at Renishaw Hall in Derbyshire. Waugh's diaries report that, standing on the terrace, Sir George Sitwell stood silently, gazing out across the valley. Eventually, he turned and spoke to Evelyn 'in the wistful, nostalgic tones of a castaway, yet of a castaway who was reconciled to his own company. Ignoring the settlement in the mining valley nearby, its streets packed with terraced housing, Sir George declared, "There is no one between us and the Locker-Lampsons."'

The story used to resonate, not only with snobs who found themselves 'marooned' in the country, but also with artsy former Londoners who were desperate for intellectual communion with others on their wavelengths. And for these former Londoners too, even in the Home Counties, there was invariably 'no one' between them and a single soulmate 30 miles away.

Yet country life has changed since Giles and I swapped stimulation for space, fresh air and lower outgoings 30 years ago. But we were in the privileged position of being able to work from home since Giles was, in theory, an artist and I a writer, so we didn't need to go into London. I, however, with my social appetite, actually did need to go there to satiate it and so I did, at least one night per week.

When we first came to Wiltshire, businesspeople had to reside in the city, except for at weekends. Forty years ago, one man commuted from Pewsey station into London. He was known as 'the commuter' and was the laughing stock of the village. Two decades later, pre-Covid, when inner London traffic had got so bad that it took as long to get into Mayfair from Pewsey station as it did from, say, Balham, suddenly Pewsey station platform was standing-room only.

Meanwhile Faversham in Kent, with its 500 buildings listed by English Heritage, has been colonised by artists and musicians who were formerly 'Swinging Londoners'. The last train to Faversham leaves London at 11.25pm so the *vieillesse dorée*, former jazz musicians, antique dealers and 1960s models who have colonised the town can have their social cake and eat it. The town has an online magazine, Faversham Life, launched in 2016, and has published more than 120 articles on an astonishing variety of topics. With 1,800 subscribers it is a testimony to the lively cultural scene in this ancient market town. Says its editor, Amicia de Moubray, 'It has become a cultural centre over the last decade or so. Lots of young couples moving in from London: fast train links, grammar school, amble to walk into country without getting in a car. Thriving musical scene.

'Downside: indigenous young people being priced out of property market.'

Marlborough, which already had a Waitrose, has become dramatically more fashionable with a Rick Stein restaurant whose public-spirited landlord let them off the rumoured to be £200,000-a-year rental when they couldn't operate during Covid. We have the haven of the four-storeyed White Horse Bookshop, which also boasts an artist's materials basement, and an art gallery, an Oxfam bookshop, two schools which offer classical concerts to the townspeople, and a jazz and literary festival. Marlborough College, where Kate, the Princess of Wales, learned how to be ladylike, curiously buys its school books direct from a distributor, rather than supporting the White Horse Bookshop whose very existence in the town helps to boost the academic credibility of the College.

A luxury cinema has now been built in the shell of an old Methodist chapel, where cinemagoers can loll back in first-class airline-type seats with a glass of wine in their hands. No longer any need to take the treacherous A346 to the freezingly air-conditioned cinemas in the Swindon hellplex. The cinema was the only thing missing in Marlborough. Now, in theory, no need to ever go to London again. Moreover, whom would we see there now so many have relocated to the country to work from home? *Urbe in rus.* Giles's hermit status is endangered. With the new influx there will soon be actually *too many people* between us and the 'Locker-Lampsons'.

Will these relocators ever go back?

Yes, is my view – if they are under the age of 45. There is an increasing number of cases of 'buyer's remorse' being talked about in relocator circles. Relocators were misled by the glorious weather of lockdown one, the space and the minimal noise and crime in the country. Moreover, of course, there was no FOMO because doing interesting or glamorous things had been banned. Might as well do nothing in a beautiful landscape than in an urban one.

But country conditions are very different now to what they were during lockdown one. I personally first ventured nervously back into the city after 18 months in the company of only a handful of others, when I attended three London parties in July 2021. They were professional, media parties. I had been fearful of being infected and unconfident about socialising because of lack of practice, but at each one of them I found the atmosphere positively euphoric as it might be at an evangelical church service and I realised that, like me, my fellow party attenders had suddenly realised what had been missing. We were like plants who needed to be watered, and it was the company of other people which was metaphorically supplying the 'water'.

A financial journalist I know, aged 65, has given up his sprawling country estate in Yorkshire and swapped it for a Mayfair flat which, he says, in its entirety could fit into the entrance hall of his former home. But thinking logically he realises that, as a single man in his sixties who is now interested more in socialising than in property status, he will do better to relocate back to the city where he knows there will always be an acquaintance passing through and needing somewhere to stay for the night. 'In later life people don't have the energy to trek across the country to see each other. But even rurally committed people always need to go to London at some time of the year. And they now know I have a spare bedroom in London so I can see them here.'

A property expert, writing in the *Spectator*, advised, in May 2021, that those who own commercial property in cities should think again before assuming they should sell up on the grounds that working from home would be the future – an idea at that time even being encouraged by the government.

He warns of arrogance. Yes, the better off may well enjoy working just as efficiently from their spacious country houses. Why commute if you don't need to? Working from home is a nice idea, as Mrs Thatcher said of Socialism, but it doesn't take account of human nature.

Anyone with office experience knows that presenteeism trumps competence. The complacent classes on their high salaries may prefer to work from their pools in Farnham, Surrey, but the junior, more dynamic employees don't want to work in their suburban bedsits. They want the space of the office and the 'vibe' of central London, and they want to socialise – even if flirting is now banned in the workplace. These juniors will work as many days as possible in the office and there they will band together and plot the overthrow of their smug, married seniors.

Yet, as Patrick the carpenter has pointed out, few people are moving house any time soon so it currently looks as though we will be permanently surrounded by the same cast of characters. If a cottage, originally built one brick thick as shelter for agricultural labourers, does come up, it is immediately moved into by someone from the middle classes, observes another local, and that started happening around 2015. The middle classes have to cut their coat according to their cloth. The big houses (which includes old rectories) start at £2.5 million, the middle-sized houses £900,000, the cottages £500,000. Renting a three-bed cottage is now £1,200 per month. One landowner puts her cottages up on Facebook when they become vacant and invites potential renters to 'bid' for them. The person who offers the highest price gets the cottage.

A 60-year-old who came to the Kensington house of my old friend Anne the other day noted, 'Your generation, the Boomers, have wonderful spacious houses; my generation has houses about a third of this size and our children have rented basements.'

Well, when Anne got her wonderful house the population on earth was 4 billion, it is now 8 billion – there are not enough houses to go round. The grandchildren of Boomers who don't want to live in London basements are relocating to the country, where they are paying more than indigenae can afford to rent cottages.

One relocator, whose own childhood home was three times the size of the cottage she is in now, says, 'The worse thing is, where do you put your coat and boots when your front door opens directly into the cottage from the street? Also I have to drive along the road and park and sit in the car to have Zoom calls with my psychotherapist.' Otherwise her boyfriend would hear everything she said.

Decamping and Country Properties

MARY:

A local property came up to rent at £800 per month and, out of nosiness, we joined a junior friend and went to have a look. It was a shock when we walked straight through the door and into a kitchen, the size of two double beds, a reception room the size of four double beds, a spacious upstairs bathroom, a quite nice bedroom the size of three double beds and another 'bedroom' slightly larger than a single bed but with a sloping ceiling. All three upstairs rooms had sloping ceilings, in fact, because they had been harvested out of the roof space. The cottage was originally a one-storey barn. Ever since, I have considered my own cottage to be large and sprawling.

In the summer months a friend's grandson came to stay in the grottage to get some work experience. Giles says that James's job only involves listening to me holding forth, almost like a paid companion. There is some truth in that but I find it helps me to have a captive audience as I try to think things through. I have to pay someone to listen because Giles and our daughters are invariably too busy to hear me out.

GILES:
The problem is that Mary tends to start whatever anecdote she is telling with the day she was born and I can't really put in the man hours to listen.

MARY:
James, who, like me, has no driving licence, has also been helping with an art exhibition in a village six miles away, and to this end Giles drove him to and fro each day. James sat silently in the gallery while on some days no one with any intention of purchasing visited the show. Still, he enjoyed the human interaction with the locals of that village.

It was a delight to have his enthusiastic company. The poor young fellow has spent two years at the University of Glasgow without attending one real-life lecture (because of Covid). For most of this time he was in isolation and forbidden to leave his student lodgings except for a walk and to go to the shops. He got a lot of reading done but he obviously feels cheated of the human experience enjoyed by every other student in the generations before him.

When Giles and I decamped to the country, in our early thirties, it was largely for financial reasons. I was not, at that point, tired of London. Now James, only in his early twenties, is already ready to leave London – but not for financial reasons. His parents have a large and comfortable house in Notting Hill Gate.

'What draws you to the city as a young person is the sense of being alive,' James says. 'The sense of buzziness, the sense of trepidation and that you are setting out on an adventure. Feeling part of something, knowing how to survive and what to do if a crackhead runs at you, gives an odd sense of satisfaction.

'But I have discovered that I like being in the country because it is so peaceful here. You don't feel like you have to do something just because your friends are all doing it. Sometimes it's useful to be able to say you can't do something because you are in the country.

'During lockdown I became an absolute master of being able to while away 15 waking hours. I joined the London Library and they were very good about posting books out to the country. It was wonderful to have the freedom to read 200 pages a day [he is a literature student].

'When lockdown ended I was no longer able to have at least ten hours a day to spend reading, or even just to myself. I now find myself going out to things in London again all the time when I would rather not. I can't think of a good enough excuse not to join in. But while I am staying with you I can just say, "Sorry, I'm in the country, working."'

I was rather pleased to think our village was peaceful – it is, largely because of the absence of traffic noise and because there aren't any noisy louts in any of the cottages.

Revelling in James's observation that we live in a peaceful and quiet village I led him, one summer's evening, on a secret walk along unmarked, although permissive, paths to give Merlin some exercise. I was babbling away to my captive audience when a series of ear-piercing screams punctuated by groans of pain rent the air. Our hearts sank. Clearly someone was in the process of being murdered.

Had there been signal I would have dialled the police.

Then I saw Rambling Bertha, an indigenous villager, walking towards us. She laughed when I asked what the noise was. 'That will be Clive Sanderson on his tennis court,' she explained. 'They always shout like that when one of them is near winning.'

The Sandersons continued to play tennis during Covid. Obviously the players stood at a great distance from each other but it was frowned upon by some villagers who thought they might transfer Covid via handling the tennis balls. Fair enough. I myself can remember spray bleaching the Amazon parcels when they were dropped off. In the early days, we did not realise that Covid was transmitted via breath.

A Mini Break to the Cotswolds

GILES:

The dream of Arcadia first came to England with the Renaissance revival of the Classics. It had its roots in Greece where Arcadia is still a real place in the Peloponnese. A wilderness in an untouched state of nature. An ideal land that city people dreamed of.

In the 20th century it had its own renaissance in the fantasies of the artist Rex Whistler, who was very fond of Wiltshire. His friend and admirer Cecil Beaton was another 'influencer' from the 20th century who sought an Arcadian bolthole in Wiltshire's Chalke Valley and brought his friends down from London to role play living in the past.

The hippies in the seventies often wanted to get back to the land because their sensitivities, following the use of mind-expanding drugs, could not cope with all the 'vibes' in the city, but these made up only a tiny percentage of escaping urbanites. The relocation trend started in the 1980s when young parents saw that they could swap a four-bed house on a noisy road in Clapham for an old rectory in the country.

The latter-day so-called 'race for space', which set off a rustic property boom, started with Covid and only following the chaotic scenes of autumn 2022 began to show signs of buckling under the higher interest mortgage rates. We may be witnessing many of those who panic-bought properties online, sight unseen, in the pandemic diaspora, now beginning to suffer buyer's remorse.

Yet the fact remains, the countryside is less stressy than the town. Researchers from the University of Glasgow recently found that when natural space in a local area rose by 10 per cent there was a corresponding fall — of 7 per cent — in early deaths amongst the under 65s.

The definitions of natural space in this study included woodland, trees, scrub, marsh, heath, open water and roadside verges, but included two categories which, in my book, are anything but natural, i.e. farmland and grass sports pitches. I am surprised that golf courses were not also included.

The wife and I had an unexpected six-day half-term window of opportunity in late October of 2022 to get away from the grot in our own grottage before winter set in and into another person's cottage — like washing up, it could never be as bad as your own, we reasoned.

Mary had been touting the possibility of a Euro break to Antwerp where the works of my favourite artist, the little-known James Ensor, are newly presented in the Royal Museum of Fine Art, which has reopened after an unfathomably long refurbishment period lasting 11 years.

Yet, having suffered a Kafkaesque ordeal involving Passenger Locator Forms during an earlier break to Paris, in February 2022, I was still nursing a grudge against 'abroad' in general. We had been made to feel like illegal immigrants in limbo in the Gare du Nord terminal and had to run in an undignified manner towards our designated Eurostar carriage.

I had also been put off abroad by a 'Tyranny of Choice' advert in a Sunday paper headed WHICH UNSPOILT GREEK ISLAND?' in a shouty typeface. A friend pointed out, 'It would be a shame if you ended up not going anywhere because you couldn't decide where to go.'

Perhaps we could find a more manageable destination in England itself? So the issue then became to WHICH UNSPOILT ENGLISH COUNTY? might we relocate to for our half-term break.

What followed was a frantic and frankly desperate exercise as we looked at Airbnbs, pubs, guest houses, boltholes and hideaways in up to five neighbouring counties, not forgetting those recommended by Alastair Sawday or by the new *Wild Guides*. The latter cater for the Instagram generation so that no haunt of ancient peace should remain in that state, for cavalcades of Chelsea tractors are now a daily feature, we are told, of the narrow lanes on Dartmoor. The occupants are on a mission: they want to jump out and gurn for selfies against the contorted and stunted trees of Wistman's Wood. The *Lord of the Rings*-style background scenery for their selfies means that Wistman's Wood may soon have to be barricaded with razor wire to protect its delicate ecosystem from the increasing footfall of the dreaded Instagrammers.

MARY:

I entreated Giles to stop negging and try to take a positive attitude towards our mini break, to think of places that are nice, not to start listing all the places that have been spoilt.

GILES:

This was not the time for me to throw a spanner in the works and submit that *most* southern counties have been more or less spoilt – thanks to the Common Agricultural Policy – by intensive agriculture.

In the post-war countryside of the 20th century, Cecil Beaton and Rex Whistler might have been able to look across a chequerboard pattern of agreeable small fields, dotted with elms and mature trees with huge crowns in an almost parkland setting – complete with shepherds wearing traditional smocks, who may or may not have been playing on panpipes to their flocks. Today, as country visitors have now realised, the threat is not so much from infrastructure and new towns as the changes resulting from the intensification of agriculture itself, in the wholesale destruction of traditional countryside, painfully recorded in former planner Marion Shoard's polemic *The Theft of the Countryside*, written in 1980. The blurb says:

The unique character of the English countryside is being
destroyed by a far-reaching agricultural revolution.
The traditional patchwork of field, down, hedge,
wood and stream which has delighted the world, is in
the early stages of a process of transformation. If it
continues unhindered, rural England will eventually
become a featureless expanse of prairie and grass
monoculture; our landscape will come to look more like
that of the American midwest or Soviet central Asia.

It is now widely understood that the engine of destruction for these changes was the Common Agricultural Policy making it profitable for farmers to turn the countryside into a vast food factory, using up every square 'hectare' of possible growing land and turning their backs on mixed farming, i.e. livestock and arable. This had hardly changed since the Neolithic era but obeyed the rule of return: that everything that was grown that could not be made use of would be returned to the land in a virtuous cycle for the maintenance of fertility. This was before bag nitrogen could be conjured out of the air.

But what farmer could resist the financial incentives? It was not the farmers that went wrong – it was the system. The farmers, unless they had private income to enable them to practise 'enlightened' farming, had to follow the money to survive.

Yet one is conflicted because, the CAP, having been the original engine of destruction, in recent years had come up with a species-recovery budget that prioritised certain birds and animal species in a collective Euro effort to stem biodiversity losses.

Eventually policies changed from isolated areas to a more joined-up approach with the idea of wildlife corridors, landscape-scale nature recovery plans and bee corridors to allow species to adapt to climate change so that they could move through the landscape, an idea which aspired to have a mosaic of different habitats.

At the time of writing I assume the monies will no longer be there to support these schemes. And if Jacob Rees-Mogg has his way with his proposed 'bonfire of green blob regulations', environmentalists will be competing with the needs of the NHS, social care and the military, which will be seen to be more urgent.

That is not to say that there aren't pockets of paradise to be found within these wrecked counties.

These pockets have sometimes been preserved by being in proximity to National Parks or conservation areas. They may be on the estates of enlightened landowners, who wish to achieve a more equitable balance between wild and productive land. They may be rich enough to turn their land over to rewilding. They may have wetlands that they choose to leave undrained.

What would the world be, once bereft
Of wet and of wildness? Let them be left,
O let them be left, wildness and wet;
Long live the weeds and the wilderness yet.
GERARD MANLEY HOPKINS, FROM 'INVERSNAID'

Marriage is a compromise and I knew that there was a chance of finding a pocket of perfect unspoilt countryside to visit at the back of the Malvern Hills. I had an image still etched in my mind, from Ken Russell's definitive 1962 biopic *Elgar*, of the young Elgar cantering along the spine of this evocative range. There were also the scholarly associations with Langland's *Piers Plowman*, whose narrator has his hilltop dream in the Malvern Hills.

I wanted somewhere rough and uncultivated, and I enlisted our daughter Fleur, fluent in the ways of the internet, to use her skills as a locations researcher. She found an isolated white cottage sitting adjacent to the spine of the Malverns, which was available to rent. Mary and I prefer to make decisions by a process of elimination. This new tendency may have resulted from our having to view so great a number of television programmes that are based on the elimination process – *Bake Off*, *Strictly*, *Love Island*, *The Masked Singer/Dancer* and most Saturday shiny-floor programmes.

In other words, when faced with a tyranny of choice we prefer it if life itself narrows the choice, rather in the spirit of John Lennon, who sang about life happening while you are making other plans. Hence we were pleased when our daughter wailed dramatically that the cottage she had found for us had gone. She chastised us for not seizing the chance to book it the moment it had become available – now it had been taken by other competitors in the race for space.

'Calm down, dear,' I said. 'That makes our job of choosing somewhere easier, not more difficult, as it is one less choice to tyrannise us.'

Besides, I had noticed that as Mary, who experienced the Troubles first hand, was viewing the pictures of the property, an anxious look had spread over her face.

She was already envisaging a situation where splendid isolation could suddenly backfire.

The chances of Mary and my landscape choices intersecting like a Venn diagram became more and more unlikely as we both had wildly different priorities. I think Mary would have been just as happy in a village setting, where she could indulge her Miss Marple fantasies, with a manageable number of cast members including a milkman, postman, clergyman, various widows and a grudge-bearing gardener.

Mary fancies herself as a student of human nature. But as a connoisseur of landscape, rather than of humanity, my brief was far more exacting. I wanted to find a cottage or 'site' in a landscape 'free of ecological wounds', to quote one of my pioneering heroes, Aldo Leopold. It is also a phrase often repeated by the doyenne of rewilding, Isabella Tree.

I wish to escape permanently from our compromised landscape to an Arcadian rough land that, unfortunately, I cannot be sure still exists. It may exist in the Shropshire Hills, or somewhere even more remote like Exmoor.

And so I realised that with our two wildly differing wish lists, one of us would have to give way to the other in order that the Venn diagram could intersect and, to quote Tony Blair, the kaleidoscope which was in flux could fall into place. Otherwise we would risk our six-day window of freedom collapsing in a bad-tempered recrimination that too much research had taken place.

MARY:

Giles has an epistolary relationship with our mutual friend Cressida. For some reason they both seem to enjoy the use of clichés and convey about 500 words of weekly news to each other using as many clichés as they can. Bless/ You couldn't make it up/I'd kill for a cuppa, etc. Giles had emailed Cressida to say we were looking for somewhere to have a 'get away from it all mini break. Break from what? You may well ask ...' etc., and Cressida emailed me to say her niece had a cottage to rent in the Windrush Valley. I went on Instagram; it looked just what we needed, clean empty rooms in minimal good taste, nooks, a wooden staircase and a log burning stove.

I thought I should bring the tyranny of choice to an end. Giles was turning what should have been a positive into a negative and I would just insist we went there.

GILES:

When I heard that Mary had finally settled for a former National Trust cottage in Windrush in the Cotswolds my heart sank, because I knew I would have to substitute my own desire for wild country for mild country, and possibly risk finding prim fields there.

But the price was right. Besides, having lived for a year in my youth in the famous Cotswold village of Adlestrop, immortalised by Edward Thomas, I had been used to purchasing my groceries from Stow-on-the-Wold. I had, so to speak, been there and bought the T-shirt.

I had grown out of that clean-shaven, slightly twee landscape with its assortment of pretty Cotswold villages and its mellow honey-coloured dry-stone walls and stone mushrooms and Teletubby equestrian areas set aside for Pony Club activities. Indeed, it's a landscape beloved now of retired sports commentators, supermodels, actresses and TV presenters. But the window of opportunity was closing and I went along with it.

The first thing I noticed, on arriving in the Cotswold village of Windrush, was just how many properties now have electronic entrance gates with intercom and blinking dial pads set into stone turrets. These electronic surveillance systems strike the wrong note – a note of absenteeism. I expect that if you have made enough new money to buy a Cotswold stone property, your first instinct is to turn your back on the world and pull up the metaphorical drawbridge, i.e. shut the electronic gates.

Death is a great leveller and although mixed ranks will presently lie alongside one another in the village graveyards, the chance of any indigenous villagers ever being able to afford one of these properties is minimal. For so many decades, they were affordable to all – the old schoolhouse, the old smithy with their quaint addresses suggesting a time when villages functioned as organic interdependent or even feudal entities, but the temptation to shut out the world must be high for these novices who know nothing of feudal life – these people who can afford to buy produce in boutique artisanal independent farm shops, much of it imported from sunnier climes in France or Italy, such as Sicilian lemons still with leaf attached, to show it has not been grown in a greenhouse in Thanet, Kent.

But 'always get over a stile,' exhorted Wiltshire writer Richard Jefferies. So, sure enough, having put my reservations about the Cotswolds on to a back boiler, I set out from our Cotswold *gîte* on a modest expedition to explore some commendably messy-looking National Trust farmland on the footpath from Windrush to the neighbouring village of Sherborne.

This is a path that meanders and skirts the River Windrush which, according to our host who lived in the next-door cottage, was famously polluted, like most rivers in England. As ex-pop star Feargal Sharkey, now punching above his weight as spokesman for River Action, points out, today the pollution is unlikely to come from industry but from agricultural emissions, e.g. nitrates from field run-off and pollution from livestock production.

It looked all right to me – the water was clear in the shallower sections and I almost disrobed, on the mild, late October day, to take the plunge. I employ the same strategy as I do with past-its-sell-by-date produce in the fridge. I use one of the few blessings with which nature has bestowed me – my perfumier's sense of smell; if there's an absence of rank odours, then this so-called wild swimmer rarely misses the opportunity for a river dip by closing nostrils and preventing the ingress of water, but that is what skin is for – it shields us from life's pollutants.

The green weeds were swaying and sashaying in a most beguiling and hypnotic manner, forcing me to abandon thoughts of the incredibly concerning news – the break-up of the Tory party, the dangerous situation in Ukraine and the avowed intent of China to reclaim the territory of Taiwan, all combining to taser my brain into submission and into a condition of abject fear that we are one miscalculation away from nuclear Armageddon ...

MARY:

Back in February 2022, I decided to give myself a news blackout. As a child in Northern Ireland, I cringed in fear of the Troubles taking place around me and the constant threat of random bombs or gunfire aimed, as so often was the case, at the wrong target. For example, a typical lead story on the evening news would be 'A schoolteacher was killed this afternoon by masked men in an unidentified car. The man had been washing up at his kitchen sink in Portadown. The security services say it appears to be a case of mistaken identity.'

Then I moved to London and cringed in fear each day as I walked to work past Chelsea Barracks – expecting them to be blown up. Then I was frightened of being 'spiked' with acid by a prankster at a drinks party. After that I was frightened of one of my parents dying. Then I was frightened of the Iraq War and then of its repercussions. Finally I was frightened of Covid.

By the time the Ukraine War came around I couldn't believe that a man of Melvyn Bragg's wisdom was watching it as rolling news. I was in the same team as Anthony Horowitz, writer of *Foyle's War*, who declared he had given himself a news blackout because this was a war we were being expected to watch in 'real time'. Watching in itself would be a form of depravity.

I do know what is going on – but only through reading the *Knowledge* and the *Week* and listening to podcasts like *The Rest Is Politics* with Rory Stewart and Alastair Campbell ('two old men talking', as my godson, 22, who works in politics, describes them). No way would I subject myself to two hours of rolling horrors per day – as Giles does. If Putin is going to nuke me – let him. I'm not going to let him have even more satisfaction by cringing in anticipation of the nuking until he does so.

GILES:

... But the gift of the fascination of watching these swaying fronds of the subterranean weeds was in its ability to bring me into that blessed state of Now, of the Present Moment, which Eckhart Tolle, in his bestselling self-help book *The Power of Now*, says should be the ideal state for human consciousness. Tolle advises you to free yourself of the fear of the future or the regrets of the past and concentrate on the moment, the only one you have power over, and stop the taser of fear infecting your life.

It reminded me of a scene in Russian film director Andrei Tarkovsky's *Solaris* – one of my favourite films. In this, he lets the camera linger on the subterranean fronds against the haunting background of Bach's *Ich ruf zu dir, Herr Jesu Christ*, played on the organ as our hero, psychologist Kris Kelvin, ponders the sacred meaning of his homeland and farm, this to emphasise that the homeland, or the motherland to Russians, takes on an almost holy reverence. How despicable it would be to tarnish all Russian culture by conflation with the ambitions of Putin.

One of my objections to where we live in Wiltshire is that we live on a steppe and that the River Avon can be found at the bottom of the valley but that all water in the chalky or greensand soils simply disappears. There are no streams, but, just occasionally in the increasingly wet winters, I can enjoy flooded fields.

In prehistoric times, according to Richard Mabey in *The Common Ground*,

> *continuously wet habitats – marshes, fens, bogs, lakes, streams and rivers – accounted for most of the low lying land that was not wooded.*

> *Although moisture is essential to the growth of all plants, no conventional British food crop will flourish in waterlogged ground. The aim of modern drainage is to keep water on the move and, ideally, to reduce wetlands to a minimum. Farmers regard water which hangs about on the top of the soil as a nuisance.*

And so it is the job of the intensive farmer to drain the fields and move water away from cultivated land. Hence I am starved of the noises of streams and rivers at home and so I was loving walking next to this river and, in its shallower sections, enjoying the rushing water, reminiscent of the babbling brooks of Scotland or the Lake District.

The 'music' of the river or even a stream is something completely absent from my own village. The only time we hear it is during increasingly frequent flood events when the rain pours off the fields and washes off the topsoil. However, usually these events are not very restful as we have to move our cars on to higher ground and cannot therefore associate the gurgling with elevated thoughts of a poetic nature.

MARY:

Why do you always have to list things that are wrong, rather than things that are right? Nowhere is perfect. I think you just like grumbling.

GILES:

Hold your horses, Mary ...

Neither was the landscape twee beyond the *Shell Guide*-neat domestic scenery of the villages. Bored of the prescribed footpath, I found myself meandering towards a marshy scene where I startled a white egret and a snipe. The snipe, in lowland England, used to be a common bird of undrained marshy land beloved of Gerard Manley Hopkins and it simply cannot abide human company. Its presence therefore acts as an emblem of wildness, a tick box in our tick-box world. I was pleasantly surprised that the Cotswolds could deliver a snipe.

I felt vaguely guilty about startling it but the satisfaction I gained from seeing it in its shy retreat justified the guilty emotion by a factor of ten to one. Admittedly I have always had a sense of entitlement. Thankfully most ramblers are law-abiding and will stick to the footpath with its newly planted hedgerow of little botanical interest.

I didn't swim because the thought of a rambler having to stumble across a half-naked overweight man, whose wife has now forbidden him to drink beer, was off-putting. And the footpath, although quiet now, could at busier moments, such as during half-term which we were in the middle of, suddenly give way to a procession of people. We live on an overcrowded island now, largely made up of solitude seekers.

Late October often brings unseasonal warm days stolen from summer. They are a stimulus to red admiral butterflies, wasps and hornets, which become active and hover drunkenly over rotting windfall apples. There were even, to my delight, a handful of field mushrooms to add to my tick box of satisfaction with this little pocket of the Cotswolds.

No, I cannot find fault with or belittle this pleasant walk in the country between Windrush and Sherborne. It is mercifully free of multicoloured trees that look like lollipops or 'zebra hedges' that alternate purple-leaved foliage with regular green. It is as good-looking as lowland English scenery gets and I would not hesitate to get out my easel and paints to record it.

The presence of many willow trees, with their untidy and wayward habits of dropping branches and succouring (sending out fresh shoots), will serve as a constant reproach to recently arrived tidy-minded landowners, whose only mission is to 'improve' the landscape with a mind-boggling assortment of sit-on mowers, leaf blowers, trimmers and other power tools.

Unearthing the Past

GILES:

Were I a shrub, I would say I have only tentatively put down roots here in Wiltshire. These relatively fresh roots are not yet thick or stubborn enough to stop me uprooting myself for the final chapter of my life.

Like some ungrateful, adopted child, I see myself as having been literally transplanted roughly from Essex by my wife and, after 30 years, I am reaching peak restlessness. I am now ready to transplant myself, this time to the 'right side' of the Long Mynd in Shropshire – although the jury is out as to whether there is a right or wrong side of this range of hills.

My sister, an amateur psychoanalyst, urges caution in my rush to blame a county for what might be shortcomings in my psychological hinterland. Might it be a form of projection of my own shortcomings? 'Know thyself' is the great religious injunction, Furthermore, Mary says she is done with moving. In other words she's dunroamin' and, if I go, I will be roamin' alone.

Yet for me the move would be easy. I have told Mary I have no allegiances to the county and do not want to be buried in the local churchyard, chiefly because of its overzealous mowing regime, which I can observe from our cottage window. Ergo, I don't want to be strimmed for eternity.

The only attachments I have formed are to my own garden and a small patch of local downland where I have a reasonable chance of not being sprayed. The internationally famous naturalist, ecologist and extinction expert Peter Marren walked with me in this patch and declared that my local bio-region was almost unique in supporting three chalkland specialist blue butterflies at the same time, namely the chalkhill blue, the Adonis blue and the common blue.

But even the downs do not escape my reservations. They don't go on and on like they used to: they end up in a ploughed field or stubble. Or a grain drying silo. The downs have lost their wilderness role. I learned that from reading Marion Shoard's angry *Theft of the Countryside*. In fact, the only full wilderness left in Wiltshire is Salisbury Plain, which has escaped cultivation only on account of it being a military training area. Reports come from birdwatching friends, who know their way about the Plain (it can be lethal if you don't know the schedules of army manoeuvres), of rare glimpses of stone curlews, short-eared owls and hen harriers to name but a few of our scarcer bird species, along with the migratory and evocatively named whinchat. As young local naturalist Arthur Heywood observes, 'Wildlife has been shepherded into tiny islands; fragments that are not connected and hard to find. But if you find them, you can experience the natural world waiting in the wings.'

Another migrant to the county was the poet, critic and naturalist Geoffrey Grigson – by all accounts a liverish and bad-tempered fellow – who moved to Wiltshire in later life. In his slim 1950s volume, *The Wiltshire Book*, he points out that Londonised counties press upon it from the east – Berkshire and Hampshire – while to the south, Southampton, Poole and Bournemouth boast prime examples of suburban ribbon development.

And yet he added, 'So Wiltshire has a delightful emptiness, a landscape windy and suggestive, stimulating and soothing.' To a landscape painter, the farmed landscape is not designed to please the eye, it's all about efficient farming. It is a landscape fit for alien abduction and it's no accident that crop circles appear regularly in the pristine wheat fields.

Only when the crop sprayer has made a mistake do you see any variation in the monotonous monoculture. Then a scarlet gash of red poppies suddenly glimmers in the cornfield! Corn marigolds, corn cockle, cornflowers. Normally these only grow in a row in my own garden from a packet named Cornfield Mix from the garden centre.

Only land that is too steep for a tractor to remain upright is saved from the plough so there is a strange effect when looking at hills in Wiltshire. They are not steep on each side but, when seen from afar, they often resemble a series of breaking waves – yet only the steep, inward-curving, falling bit of the wave, as ridden by the surfer. *That* part is uncultivated and calls to mind the long pause while the surfer is waiting patiently for the right wave.

There is no respecting the land's natural contours but the massive cultivating machines act like a giant tongue, greedily licking the land as if it were an ice cream and sometimes allowing itself to slurp even on to the sacred herb-rich turf of hills, the best walking country in the world.

The land, in a more enlightened period in some unspecified future, will need to be reconsecrated, perhaps by a cohort of American First Nation shamans using peyote with appropriate healing incantations and much ceremony.

The real engine of destruction was the afore-mentioned Common Agricultural Policy, which met-astasised our green and pleasant land almost into submission. But I am not, like George Monbiot, in the market of demonising conventional farming. I find hope in the fresh green shoots of a movement loosely called

'Regenerative Farming'. After all, farming always used to be regenerative until bag nitrogen replaced the time-honoured 'rule of return'.

But back to Grigson. 'If Wiltshire, under its white clouds, is so markedly prehistoric, it is also markedly English,' he wrote. The greater part of Wiltshire is a platform of chalk covered by a light flinty soil. Here, on the Marlborough Downs, Salisbury Plain and Cranborne Chase, the early settlers found no forest to be cleared. There was scrub, perhaps, but this country of sky and distance and gently rolling slopes was good for cattle, pigs and sheep, and for a primitive agriculture at a time when most of Britain was hidden by a tangle of oak. So from a very early time before 2000 BC and for more than a thousand years to come, Wiltshire was the cultural heart of Britain.

Writing before the arrival of the M4, Grigson referred to these overlooked areas as 'the green vacuum of Wiltshire', meaning that the great British routes tended to bypass the county as it swept folk down to Devon and Cornwall.

Green vacuum. That phrase struck me forcibly when I read it.

Mary asks what I have been doing for the last 30 years, 'apart from taking endless routine tests at the surgery and always returning with a clean bill of health?'

She may well ask. But I have been slowly and painstakingly filling that green vacuum of my former wheat field. They say nature abhors a vacuum so when, on arrival, I was faced with not even a bush to shelter behind in our one acre, I have been addressing the main collateral damage of Common Agricultural Policy, namely loss of character. I have been replacing monoculture with polyculture, a complex mosaic of closed canopy, scrub and grassland habitats. To clarify, what I am doing is fagoting, pollarding, coppicing, mulching, bastard trenching and mob grazing. With mob grazing, I use my own hobnail boots to replicate the action of innumerable hooves of ruminants. It involves stamping on dead twigs and discarded brash to pulverise woody matter and disturb the ground to create a revitalised soil. These aforementioned actions would ideally create ecological niches for natural regeneration, first by ground flora and their associated assemblages of invertebrates and, inevitably, fungi.

Of course, I needn't have bothered. As James Lovelock, another incomer to the county like Grigson and me, discovered, left to its own devices land almost inevitably turns gradually into woodland without the aid of plastic tree shelters. But I couldn't wait. Perhaps if I had owned more than one acre, I could have allowed nature to do its own thing as it is famously doing at Knepp Castle in railway sidings.

While I admire Grigson's scholarship, he was very rude about the supreme interpreter for the whole county for all time, namely Richard Jefferies (1848–87), who describes a world so different from today, but whose vision of Wiltshire resonates in the physical landscape and in the customs and traits of its indigenae.

In and out of fashion, Jefferies remains drastically underread, although it is his, not Grigson's, bust that stands in Salisbury Cathedral. He was, according to one fly jacket, 'probably the most imaginative, passionate, inconsistent and insatiably curious and the least conventional of country writers'. He did not work the land, nor did he always live in the county, and yet in his prolific output of newspaper articles, essays and novels almost all our current ideas about rural life can be found. He is also the pioneer of that format known as 'The Country Diary'.

Turning to the journal of the Richard Jefferies Society in spring 2022, I find a review of a book about English landscape titled *A Sweet View: The Making of an English Idyll* by Malcolm Andrews. Says Andrews of Jefferies, 'no single writer did more to mediate and promote the experience of English scenery and natural life by the cumulative act of flooding the reader's mind with an abundance of named natural flora and fauna of the English countryside.'

I wish I had written this myself. It perfectly encapsulates the cult-like reverence we worshippers of Jefferies regularly experience, when reading his prose.

'In terms of his deep familiarity with the many plants which were disappearing', Jefferies serves, as Andrews puts it, 'as a kind of memory bank or intellectual seed vault for the traditional English countryside.'

Indeed. One of the most surprisingly modern aspects of Jefferies is, in the late Ronald Blythe's phrase, his 'dismissal of time'. In this respect Jefferies is right on trend as recent discoveries in quantum physics confirm what mystics and scientists have long suspected, which is that time is an illusion, created by humans to help humans get through life.

The Story of My Heart, the first book I read of his, will attract or repel the reader according to their nature. In it we get an impression that Jefferies worships not a Christian god, but the sun: he is a pagan, or akin to an animist. In one essay on landscape painting he even rejects a church spire, regarding it as an intrusion into the landscape!

Blythe praises Jefferies' 'exultant, unhidden paean to nature and hymn to joy', but there is nothing sentimental in his description of country life. As for the winter, he doesn't varnish the truth. In *Hodge and His Masters*, his study of the farming world, Jefferies writes, 'The aspect of a corn-growing district in the colder months is perhaps more dreary than that of any other country scene. It is winter made visible.'

With winter rainfall at record levels it's hard to stay upright while walking the dog and so, rather than heading towards the hills, I tend to trudge disconsolately along the edge of giant ploughed fields the size of Heathrow airport.

Flints

GILES:

A winter walk in Jefferies' day might have been leavened by the cry of a flock of peewits, anything to *re-lleviate the boredom*, to use Wiltshire parlance. But, despite shovelling taxpayers' money into agri-environment schemes to get them back, ecologists submit that most agri-environment agreements are too proscriptive so peewits mostly turn up their beaks at modern farmland. It's not messy enough for them. There is no choice but to look downwards at the dull clods and, lo and behold, there's poor man's treasure in that 'dirt' in the form of worked flints, many a miracle of workmanship.

According to Jefferies, 'Beauty has no period; it comes at intervals unexpected; it cannot be fixed. No wonder the earth is at its feet.' Flint, not surprisingly, crops up everywhere in Jefferies' *oeuvre*. In a memorable passage from *Hodge and His Masters* concerning the slow and painful process of a failing farm, a large white poster is pasted on the wall of a barn with the words 'Sale By Auction' in bold print. A succession of sturdy rustic folk are described coming to inspect the notice, and then it is the turn of two urchins. 'Two boys – cottager's children – come home from school; they look round to see that no one observes, and then throw flints at the paper till the sound of footsteps alarm them.'

Flint was held in special regard by our ancestors and is generally thought to form in a deep-sea environment from silica-secreting organisms, particularly diatoms, which undergo a process of transformations. It was the dominant type of stone-tool raw material used in the British Isles during the Stone Age. The trick is in visiting museums to get your eye in and learn to distinguish between human work and natural shapes.

The inhabitants of Clun in Shropshire are lucky in having a wonderful resource for the study of assemblages of local flint tools, gathered from local collections. This is an exemplary, characterful museum which, alongside many glass cabinets of flints, houses a fine example of a mantrap of the sort seen in one of my previously described favourite films, *Straw Dogs*. If only every village had a local museum like Clun. At a time when English identity itself is under scrutiny we need to know whence we came into being so we can be as belligerent as the Scots and the Welsh. Perhaps the best analysis of the English character was made by Richard Ingrams, who claims we are Phlegmatists.

Metal detecting, birdwatching, cycling, walking ... these are all mass participation hobbies or activities with their own lobby groups. Collecting flints is a bit niche but it's waiting for someone to write a layman's Collins-style guide to flint tool types.

In an illuminating essay, Jefferies wrote,

> *The peculiarity of flint is that, if tapped in a particular manner, it chips off, or splits almost to a nicety in proportion to the strength and direction of the blow. Thus primitive man was able to make spear-heads and arrowheads, knives and so on of really exquisite workmanship and artistic shape.*

These I search for amongst the clods.

There are scrapers, awls, burins, micro-burins, axe heads, picks and perforators. The most eagerly sought item and the most elusive is an arrowhead. And with good reason. So exacting was the workmanship involved that few cavemen could afford to lose their ammo and, with powers of observation sharper than in our time, they would leave no stone unturned to retrieve them.

In the past, landowners would pay their field-faring men some paltry sum to hunt for axe heads. Consequently there are fewer to be found. They are, of course, a finite resource yet still ubiquitous, judging from the weary expressions on the faces of finds officers at the local museum when presented with yet another heap of this poor man's treasure. A wonderful 1928 pamphlet from the British Museum, titled *An illustrated manual of the Stone Age for beginners price sixpence*, suggests the fashion for flint collecting, like the reputation of Richard Jefferies, waxes and wanes.

In the final paragraph of his essay, Jefferies writes,

> *But pause – a solitary star, it is Arcturus, which Job the great poet watched and wrote of in the old world days, shines down through the elm branches and the bats are wheeling in mazy circles round the trees. It is time to go. The flint dropped from the hand on the sward rolls out into the road, to be crushed with all its marvellous history under the careless wheel of the thoughtless carter, ground into powder to the last serving man by mending his highway.'*

Some think my obsession with Jefferies has gone too far, but to my mind, as an A level student of English literature with a chip on my shoulder that I did not attend university, may I submit that there is an almost cinematic quality to his prose? The construction of his sentences has musicality and cadence; it could be set to music like Matthew Arnold's 'The Scholar Gypsy' was picked up by Vaughan Williams and presented as an effective combination of words and music in *An Oxford Elegy*.

I once found a Roman coin in my garden and got terribly overexcited. 'It must be worth something!' I yelled. Sometime later, I read in Jefferies that it is an all too common mistake made by cottage-dwelling folk to find an ancient coin and invest it with impossible dreams of riches.

Richard Jefferies, my Supreme One Interpretation Centre for living in Wiltshire.

THE POACHER

AT THE FIRST SIGN OF A GAMEKEEPER, THE POACHERS VANISH LIKE GHOSTS.

Section 5

GHOSTLY GOINGS-ON

On the paranormal, a deep cleanse
and the haunted village

GILES:

Mary and I have spent much of our lengthy relationship 'trapped under the same roof 24/7' (her words). Mary is a temperamental sort, so I have never taken too seriously her regular accusations that my multiple character faults indicate that I 'literally need to see an exorcist'.

Nevertheless, I have always been interested – in a quasi-scientific, Rupert Sheldrake sort of a way – in the paranormal. So the prospect of an 'energy and past-life healing session' conducted by chakra expert Georgia Coleridge on the cottage, and perhaps even on ourselves, piqued my interest.

Georgia's own interest had been piqued by her remote reading of a room plan of our cottage, contained in our book *The Diary of Two Nobodies*, in which she recognised the tell-tale signs of blocked energies. These might, she told Mary, typically comprise a raft of different problems including nature spirits or imprints of the moods of past personalities. You would not hire Georgia to 'cleanse' your house, or heal its energies, unless you at the very least admit the possibility of reincarnation.

'Georgia's offered to come and cleanse the cottage,' said Mary.

I immediately started channelling Kenneth Williams by suggesting that, on her arrival, I should arm Georgia with an apron, Marigolds, a bucket of bleach and a Spontex scourer, and frogmarch her into our not overly

clean kitchen. Cue Mary to interject 'NOT CLEANING …
CLEANSING … *spiritual* cleansing, you chump!'

But I went along with it. It seemed a harmless New-Agey, Gwynneth Paltrowish thing for Trustafarians. Like putting an avocado stone in a shower head to 'purify' the water. I made that up, by the way. A glance at Georgia's book *The Chakra Project*, however, pointed towards a philosophy based on ancient Indian Vedic scriptures. If these scriptures were good enough for Aldous Huxley (*The Perennial Philosophy*), they were good enough for me. Moreover the book included some more 'accessible' stuff about things like crystal worship to add to the pick 'n' mix and attract a wider contemporary audience.

The belief in ghosts is booming in spite of Richard Dawkins and modern education. In fact, ghost hunting is a popular TV genre. In the 1972 frightener *The Stone Tape*, now shockingly dated, we were first introduced to the concept of a building as a psychic tape recorder which might 'play back' traumatic events to those sensitive folk who could divine its messages. Not every soul goes to its appointed place at once. A past sin, or an undischarged duty, might hold it earthbound for a season or longer and the spirits are 'stuck' in limbo.

So I couldn't wait to get started on our ghost-busting tour of the cottage. But I didn't like it when Mary suggested I collect Georgia from a train station 40 minutes away on my own ('so she can pick up on your vibes without them being diluted by mine'). I suspected an archetypal conspiracy between females, an assumption that I, the only male present, might be the spanner in the cottage works.

I did not want my quiet life being disturbed by a full exorcism with 360-degree head turning and French profanities. Fortunately, or perhaps spookily, as I set out to Swindon, a symbol of a spanner appeared on the dashboard, forcing me to perform a U-turn and order her a taxi instead. That was a close shave.

My litmus test of any new visitor to the cottage is whether they appreciate my wild garden. Georgia insisted on a pre-prandial garden tour and, unlike another recent visitor, a friend of a friend who described it as 'horribly overgrown', she fell in love with it.

So I was well disposed when she began to perform a forensically detailed room-by-room spiritual survey, especially once I realised that unlike a dental treatment there would be no physical pain involved for myself. But there was definitely something happening. Deep yawns and gurgling noises in her stomach were clear evidence of a transformation of energies taking place in the healer's own corporeal realm.

She identified three ghosts of former occupants. None of them malign but all of them 'stuck'. One, who had sat huddled at the fireplace for many years, 'was a simple fellow, he didn't think much.' If we consider the low expectations of agricultural workers of the previous centuries, the lack of stimuli, education or even curiosity, this could only be expected.

Another was a boy of 16 (when he died). The third an old lady who had lived during Queen Victoria's reign. Georgia moved them onwards and upwards. She encouraged the boy to go to a 'country fair' and an angel came to take the very old lady.

She also expelled a cohort of nature spirits in the kitchen (where Mary and I argue the most) and I helped by enthusiastically swishing a smoking sagebrush torch in the direction of the back door, which had been opened to allow the *exeunt omnes*. How easily I took to the task while Georgia rang a pair of pinging oriental bells.

It was a singular experience and not something I am prepared to be cynical about. Something happened. Like all true mystical experiences, it would suffer from the banality of being translated into words. Suffice to say I can see why estate agents use the services of Georgia Coleridge to 'cleanse' the energies of properties that inexplicably will not sell.

MARY:

There is definitely something more ghostly about the country than the town. Why should this be?

In a town, where people come and go so much more and stay for such short times in their houses and flats, no anecdotes about hauntings get passed on. If you are selling a property obviously you would keep quiet about such things as they would be a turn-off to the suggestible. But in a rural community everyone already knows if properties are 'haunted' and an incomer will find out soon enough. When we first came to the village, Candida in the Manor Farm, who was a horsewoman, told me that whatever horse she was riding always became spooked when they arrived at a certain corner on the lane between us and the next village. Horses are intuitive, of course, but there was nothing to see there. Then Candida found out this corner was where the gibbet was positioned in the days of hanging – the evil vibes were obviously still emanating on some subatomic level.

In the Black Swan pub in Devizes there is known to be a 'fellow occupant' in room number 4. This takes the form of a young woman in a flowing dress who 'melts' in and out of the wall. The same vision has been reported by innumerable guests, some of whom leave the room in the middle of the night and wait in the downstairs restaurant until dawn before settling their bill and beating a retreat.

Others, ghost enthusiasts, deliberately book this room. It's the same in the cellar of the Black Swan where the temperatures can suddenly plunge for no good reason. Rather than covering up the hauntings, the pub has found they are good for business.

In our own village there is the legend of the Ghost of Pit Pond, a story which so intrigued Charles Dickens, he wrote about it himself. Back in 1848, the occupant of the Manor Farm, Mr Reeve, was a bachelor. We can see his house from our front windows to this day. One morning, walking on top of the downs, Reeve heard the thundering of urgently advancing hooves and saw a young girl astride a pony, galloping helter-skelter towards what he knew to be a dew pond – a piece of land that looks just like a grassy sward but in fact the grass conceals a deep chalk pit, ready for strangers to fall into.

Mr Reeve shouted a warning and, to his amazement, the quick-reacting rider somehow made the pony jump for its life, just in time, and it miraculously cleared the dew pond and landed safely on the other side.

The rider dismounted and was clearly shocked by her narrow escape so Mr Reeve and his farmworker took her down to the Manor Farm to give her a drink. The girl asked for a glass of water, but 'there was none to be had except from a jug dipped into the crystal-clear waters of the pond below the Manor Farm', reported a local worker some years after the event. This was known as the Pit Pond. 'A clear bright pool it was then, like a fountain,' said the worker. 'You could count every flint that lay at the bottom.'

As she gratefully swallowed the water the girl explained that she was part of a circus visiting the local town of Marlborough. This was why her pony had been able to perform this fantastic acrobatic feat of clearing the pond. Mr Reeve was falling in love – he said he had never before felt anything like he did for this beautiful creature, not more than 19 years old.

To his horror, a handsome young man suddenly hove into view, galloping down the hill crying, 'Emily!' Mr Reeve was relieved when the young man introduced himself as Emily's brother.

In those days, the roads were unmade and a resident of the village wouldn't venture far, yet Mr Reeve spent two happy weeks in the company of the brother and sister, growing more in love each day. Yet, cruelly, Emily and the young man were not brother and sister – they were a romantic couple but had concealed this as they were unmarried. On her last visit to the village, as he showed her his homestead and garden, Mr Reeve proposed. Mr Reeve's housekeeper, who was spying on them, said that Emily rejected the proposal. She left the area and was never seen here again.

Mr Reeve went downhill. He seemed to take no pleasure in anything other than standing at Pit Pond, looking down into the water. One day, the villagers found Mr Reeve's hat bobbing on the pond, and rakes, hooks, poles and ropes were dragged through the water but they could find nothing. However, within the threshing barn, Mr Reeve was found hanging from the beam.

After his death there were the sightings. Many villagers saw the ghost of Mr Reeve drifting about the village and eventually a community attempt was made to move the spirit on. The exorcism was performed in the biggest room in the farmhouse with five clerics and most of the village present.

Mr Reeve himself manifested at the meeting – looking just like he had in life, 'except with his head slightly to one side' and 'gurgling when he talked'. So said all the witnesses present. The clergymen asked him to stop haunting the village and Mr Reeve replied that he would only do so if he could be 'laid in the Red Sea to cool his heated soul'. One clergyman suggested the Pit Pond, with its shady chilly waters, would do as well and Mr Reeve agreed. Legend has it that he was exhumed from the village graveyard and placed in the pond, where the crystal-clear waters became immediately muddied and the horses refused to drink there any more. But the hauntings stopped.

We have often wondered where the exact location of the offending dew pond is on the top of the downs.

A Modern-Day Scare

MARY:

Last summer there was a drama in the woods. A young girl striding confidently across the downs, but following a map on her iPhone instead of the marked permissive path, walked straight into a dew pond with a thick carpet of grass floating on top and underneath a soggy bottom, which began to suck at her walking boots. She became trapped there, unable to escape and being swallowed further down with each movement.

She rang 999, but the emergency services' computer told them she was in quite a different spot to where she truly was. Wise villager Stu saw the ambulance and fire brigade arrive and, following a hunch, stopped them as they headed in the wrong direction and led them up to the dew pond on his quad bike. The girl was extracted by the use of a long pole with a hook on the end of it.

So my cautionary message is this. Don't go off a permissive path or a right of way when walking somewhere strange – or even not strange. We had been walking in those woods for decades and no one in the village, except this lone countryman, knew that the dew pond was there. Without his knowledge, the girl would have perished.

HAS ENGLISH DOWNLAND LOST ITS WILDERNESS ROLE?

Section 6

DOG WORLD

On the joys of Merlin, the terror of dog theft and an exorbitant snip op

MARY:

I know that Merlin is the main source of the dirt in the cottage (after Giles with his gardening tools left lying everywhere – 'Where are my shears? I left them on the kitchen table!') but our dog is also the most reliable source of happiness.

Every time your eye falls on him you are rewarded by a spectacle of beauty – he looks like a cross between a teddy bear and a miniature lion – and he is a constant source of positive feedback. What's most rewarding is to consider what is going on inside his head as he stares at the crackling log fire. It's consoling to have one sentient being in the cottage who knows nothing of Brexit, Covid or Putin and who is thinking only about dog walks, dog food and chasing rabbits.

Times were particularly tough for burglars during lockdown. They couldn't go to 'work' since everyone was in and some diversified into that most cruel of crimes – dog theft. Look away now if you are an easily upset dog lover.

Dog thieves, I read in *The Times*, were going online to get the names and addresses of breeders. They would then turn up, offering to clean patios with a power hose, during which activity they would do a reconnoitring mission and come back under the cover of darkness with wire-cutting tools. Tennis balls coated with liver would go into the mouths of greedy Labradors, who would then be muzzled so the dogs could breathe but not bark. Then they tied their front and back paws together and carried them away like so many handbags.

As for those who made the mistake of posting pictures of themselves on social media walking their designer dogs, they had only themselves to blame if the criminals were able to get the GPS of their locations and lie in wait along the favoured routes.

Sometimes the sign of an inexperienced dog owner is the sight of a poo bag dangling from a hedge or tree. New dog owners, when confronted, will be astonished that they have done the wrong thing. They feel that cleaning up the mess is enough and no one should expect them to travel back home with a stinking bag of dog poo in the car. The National Trust now advises that dog poo be kicked into undergrowth rather than plasticised and put into ordinary rubbish bins.

As soon as Merlin sees one of us even glance at our walking boots he goes on his hind legs dancing and panting because he longs to be in that landscape. He is epigenetically programmed to spend all day staring out at it from the window of Room 2. Trouble is, his frustration mounts as we can never find the lead.

Tibetan spaniels were bred to be working dogs. Their original role was to use their exceptional eyesight to alert the monks in the Tibetan monasteries to the arrival of strangers and to this end they always went to the highest point of the monastery where they would have the best view.

Due to the rise in dog thefts, I began the practice of walking with neighbours and their dogs so there would be safety in numbers. As long as neither of the two bitches in the village was on heat, Merlin, an intact male, could be let off the lead when we got off the road and happiness would surge through him as he ran freely into the landscape at a speed of 20 miles an hour.

Country Vets

GILES:

Now that's where, by local knowledge, a country dweller will make a good saving: vet bills. Merlin needed to go under anaesthetic to have some teeth removed and the local quote was £1,200. The figure was horrifying but a Notting Hill friend told us it was a bargain. She had paid £3,000 for the same procedure to be carried out on her cockapoo. Merlin joined a waiting list for the 'snip op'. The term 'snip op' was coined by a tabloid when Michael Parkinson became the first high-profile figure to have a vasectomy. Ever since, Mary and I have referred to all operations – even hysterectomies and amputations – as 'snip ops'. We like the expression.

I noticed during Covid that just as children have gone from being apple-scrumping nuisances whose ears needed boxing, to little emperors, boasting their own fashion ranges, so dogs, who were once called Fido or Rex and existed primarily to bring their master his newspaper or slippers, also seem to have gained the upper hand.

The dogs of our childhood were fed the tried-and-tested brands, namely Pedigree Chum, Winalot and a

Bonio rusk for variation of texture. Now there are mega-stores for pets, packed full of the most extraordinary range of products you had no idea your pooch needed – kibbled this and that, chicken-flavoured dog biscuits in the shape of chickens, dog pulls, ranges for small, inter-mediate and large dogs and with a bewildering selection of wet food, dry food, plaque-removing biscuits and not a budgie in sight.

A new dog superstore has opened up in Marlborough and I noticed a sign advertising 30 minutes free parking in its car park – which particularly appealed to me in 'Rip-off Britain' and I swung the car into a space there.

I made my purchase and crossed the road to the health centre to pick up a prescription. I found on return to the car that I had ten more minutes still to use up with the free parking. Although I am a busy man, it would never occur to me to leave early if I had ten free minutes because, as Mary has noted, I often confuse saving money with making money. I prefer to sit staring blankly and making the most of the free time in such a car park, rather than going and making more money by working.

As I sat in the car, a white-coated figure appeared at the window smiling. 'Here you are, sir,' she said, handing through a leaflet. 'We have an introductory offer for new customers. One hundred pounds for all canine dental procedures.'

I didn't tell her that Merlin was on a waiting list for a £1,200 snip op. Instead, I drove home, got Mary and Merlin in the car, and he had an assessment. A couple of days later the operation was performed (no hidden charges – it cost £100 and no more as promised), Merlin recovered fully and we breathed a huge sigh of relief.

It turned out that financial sharks in the City have seen there is money to be made out of people whose sentimentality will trump their common sense. Not only have these City firms been buying up funeral businesses, they have now set their sights on vet practices.

The new vet in Marlborough is a family-run firm, which has so far escaped the claws of the finance sharks.

The Point Of Dogs

GILES:

One of my best friends always shrinks away from Merlin when he comes to the cottage. An over-protective parent, Gerry was in the habit of taking his sons to Clapham Common where often out-of-control rumbustious large dogs would come bounding towards them, especially if a ball game was being played.

Gerry was a classic example of helicopter parenting. In my day, the child would have been taught to adopt a proportionate response and put his hands behind his back and just wait till the dog lost interest. Gerry, however, would heave the toddler on to his shoulder and, at the risk of losing his balance, kick wildly at any dog – even a chihuahua – that had come towards them. Thus he bred within his sons a lifelong fear of attack by canines.

It is hardly surprising that both boys are now cat lovers as Gerry's actions caused an early form of canine aversion therapy.

For me, the point of going for a walk with the dog is to avoid having to have a conversation. Experience has taught me that if any other villager is out, we cannot even concur on the weather. For example, if I say, 'It's mild out' (because I have a particularly effective anorak), the villager tends to shiver and reply, 'Brr, Giles, I'd say it's raw out today. This is what I call brass-monkey weather.'

To one particularly cussed villager I once ventured, with a theatrical shrug of the shoulders, what I thought was a harmless opening gambit, 'What season is this?', only to be shut down by the reply, 'I'm buggered if I know.'

For me, anyway, though not for Mary, these ex-changes tend to be remarkably unproductive. It is partly because we are living through a period of climate chaos in which all the old certainties of fixed seasons are in a state of flux.

So, therefore, unlike Mary, I prefer to walk the dog on my own and tend to keep conversations short with other dog walkers. It would never occur to me to share a route with another dog walker.

Moreover, as a biodiversity recorder and insect obsessive I tend to go on to the stewardship schemes in search of butterflies or dive on to the tramlines in crops. This I justify on the basis that I am a lot lighter than a tractor tyre and therefore cannot possibly be doing any harm. Yet I can see that to others it might seem that walking through the tramlines represents my having a 'sense of entitlement'.

We hear a lot these days about people having senses of entitlement as a consequence of having been to a public school. I went to a public school. Some say that

Shrewsbury is in the top ten of public schools but it becomes a 'minor' public school when you find yourself in a room full of Etonians, for whom there is only one school. When you hear an Etonian ask another man, 'Were you at School?' you know they are 98 per cent certain of what their answer will be. They have developed what might be called School-dar.

NEIGHBOUR FROM HELL: BARRY THE HUMAN HORNET

Section 7

THE VILLAGE COMMUNITY

On like-minded friends, the pleasures
of social intercourse, the importance of
local etiquette and village testimonies

GILES:

To those considering a move to the country — whether wild or prim — a network of close or like-minded friends who live locally, who may also be incomers, is essential if moving from the city.

These networks act as support groups or echo chambers to one's own philosophies and, at their most evolved, they can take the form of more creative communities similar to those that centred on Charleston in Sussex, e.g. the Bloomsbury Group, or the artistic community at the Benton End farm of Cedric Morris and Arthur Lett-Haines in Suffolk, or the Benjamin Britten set around the Red House in Aldeburgh.

Too late for us, the Brotherhood of Ruralists, based in Devizes, which included Graham Ovenden and David Inshaw.

A growing interest in biodiversity wildlife gardening and overcoming the 'yuck' factor to develop an interest in insects, I would recommend, should be part and parcel of moving to the countryside. As well as studying local flora and fauna, you might even become a useful member of society by becoming a biodiversity recorder, submitting your invaluable records to the Wildlife Trust or bodies such as Butterfly Conservation.

But wildlife is not for everybody. Incomers may move to the countryside to be next to a golf club or to Soho Farmhouse to play Marie Antoinette.

There are many pockets of rural Britain where a lack of like-minded fellow creatives makes the artist/writer/ musician forget about their talents and turn to drinking themselves into oblivion. This is a national problem with Finns and used to be a problem in the old priest-ridden Ireland. It is a problem with a Lancashire artist-friend of ours, who previously worked in the tradition of J.M.W. Turner, who has 'no one' living near him except a fastidious graphic designer. The influence of the latter has had a restricting effect on his paintings whose representations have now become over-exacting.

MARY:

Giles, like most older men, resists social intercourse and complains up to the point of entering the room or the guests entering the cottage – then he comes to life like a ventriloquist's dummy and clearly enjoys every second of it.

Covid and the lockdowns were the happiest period of his life. He could work all day every day in the garden with no threat of anyone inviting him to go anywhere else.

When Covid ended we were invited to London to have dinner with one of his favourite people, who also invited two more of his favourite people. I handed Giles the phone to speak to Guy, expecting him to be delighted by the invitation, but he explained to Guy that since Covid he had got out of practice with going to dinner parties and had lost the knack of talking at the same time as eating. He said that he was worried there would be a choking risk were he to attend and therefore sadly he had to decline.

One social event for which he always has enthusiasm is lunch at a pub near Devizes. Giles is ecstatically happy there and always orders 'gammon, pineapple, egg and chips'. His guests go along with it, thinking Giles must know something they don't know about this pub – 'Oh, but the menu looks pretty awful, Giles. Are you sure you want to go there?'

'Trust me,' says Giles. 'It's absolutely delicious.'

But the food always lives down to expectations and is as cardboardy and flavour-free as you might expect from ultra-processed food which has been held in a freezer for years, then thawed and heated in a microwave.

Giles particularly enjoyed going there during relaxed lockdown when we ate outside. We were all issued with throbbers on our table and, when the food was ready, the throbber would throb and then we had to walk up to a counter and collect it along with clingfilm-wrapped knives and forks.

GILES:

The TV series *Neighbours from Hell* usually features unfriendly neighbours who have fallen out over footling matters like car parking, boundaries or overhanging vegetation. Grudges have escalated from molehills into mountains so to speak. Barry, one of many temporary renters of a cottage further down the terrace, became a neighbour from hell for being too friendly.

In summer he left his front door open so he could shout a cheery greeting to passers-by. Each time I returned to the cottage he was there to ask me if I had had a good time on my trip into Pewsey – or had I been to

Marlborough? Followed by, wearing a sympathetic face, 'how *are* you Giles?' I am a fan of the traditional reserve that used to characterise the English.

Barry was also in the habit, if he caught me on my way out of the cottage, of exhorting me to 'have a nice day', or 'take care'.

He was exceptionally nosey and once I found him in my garden busy cutting my hedge with shears. 'You're welcome, Giles,' he enthused, though I had not thanked him. 'Quite honestly I had nothing better to do and I have run out of hedge in my garden.'

One day, Mary opened the front door to get the milk to find Barry standing on the doorstep with a pint in each hand. Pushing past her he said, 'I'll just put these in your fridge for you.'

Mary and I determined not to open the front door without peeping out to see who was there, but Barry outwitted us by walking into the garden and coming in through the back, holding a punnet of gooseberries he had grown. This less formal door is usually left open in the summer.

He regularly pretended that his cat was missing, which explained why I often found him wandering around my one acre garden; no inch of it went unexplored by him. In fact, I became phobic of Barry. The relief when he moved on was palpable. I had begun to have dreams about him attempting to gain ingress into our cottage in the guise of a giant hornet, tapping at our bedroom window.

MARY:

Socially, Giles loves the Wettons, whom he first met when he spied them 'trespassing' in our garden, in other words using the right of way, and went forward to challenge them. Giles took an immediate liking to Philip Wetton, who is 20 years older, and vice versa. For many years he went on holiday with Philip, a former diplomat, and Roswitha, his EU bureaucrat wife, to La Palma in the Canary Islands where they had a second home. I never went once because I didn't like the idea of scrabbling on black pebbles up the edges of volcanoes and down precipitous mountainsides to reach rocky, black-sand beaches. Moreover, I didn't fancy having to cope with Philip Wetton having blood-sugar-related hissy fits twice a day. Or the idea of his painstakingly picking *all* the almonds on an almond tree and then squashing them into an almond paste. Giles said that the main reason he liked going was that it gave him the chance to sit in the back of the Wettons' car while they drove and decided what was going to happen that day, and that it was his last chance to 'recreate the experience of being a child'.

Despite liking them so much, Giles only sees them about three times a year as he is so busy gardening. I enjoy going to their house, although to access it you have to take the road between Alton Barnes and Lockeridge, which, being a featureless and repetitive stretch of road, can be quite dangerous. It has a reputation for 'Sloanes texting and veering on to the wrong side of the road'.

I would be happy to socialise every day. Perhaps it's because, as a child, my father had his surgery in part of the house and I was subliminally primed to have 12 bits of social interaction a day. I enjoyed part one of Covid but by July 2021 I'd had enough and began to think that I might be suffering from depression for the first time in my life. Those first three post-lockdown parties in London, which I mentioned earlier, included an awards lunch at the Boisdale restaurant in London's Canary Wharf, and by then I had decided that it would almost be worth getting Covid to attend such an event with such a payload of like-minded people. From the moment I walked in, I knew I had made the right decision. My *joie de vivre* was restored within about seven minutes.

Although I had not had Covid, I still felt inexplicably tired during 2020 and 2021. Since I was no longer going to London and had completely reduced social intercourse to distanced walks with neighbours and churchyard church services, I should have had more energy not less. My feeling is that the morphic resonance theory of Rupert Sheldrake may have been pertaining. Perhaps we were somehow zoning in to the health statuses of our fellow humans. Then there's the hypervigilance theory as embraced by my friend Louise.

'As cavewomen we had to be hypervigilant if we knew there was a lion outside the cave but felt safe inside. With Covid we were hypervigilant for many months. It too was a deadly threat, but it never ended since we had no way of knowing when or whether, even if we hid inside, we might be infected ourselves. The cortisol was not just peaking in our systems occasionally, it was a permanent feature and this was physically exhausting.'

In the summer of 2021 I went to a lunch party given by Louise. We sat at a table in the garden and had roast beef and roast potatoes with Yorkshire pudding, length-sliced carrots and peas, followed by jelly croquettes with berries within the jelly. There were many dogs at the lunch and I was sorry I had not brought my own.

There were five writers, two lawyers, two farmers and one head of an Oxford college. Everyone present said they had lost their powers of concentration and could not read any more. They could only binge-watch Netflix. The lawyer yawned as he told me he had become very flaky since Covid. He said there was a time when if somebody invited him to come up to London to play a game of golf, he would get in the car and think nothing of it but now he couldn't be bothered.

Village Life and Characters

MARY:

Not being able to drive has affected my quality of life but, despite 80 lessons, I never got further than being able to drive forward, indicate and turn a corner – and only with a driving instructor with access to dual controls sitting beside me. It cheers me up that fellow non-drivers include David Attenborough, Melvyn Bragg and Brian Eno, but it means I am a prisoner except for when kind female friends pick me up and we go motoring together, using the time productively to talk things through at great length and arrive at resolutions. It's just like being in the psychiatrist's chair because you are not looking at the other person.

Since I conflate shopping with achievement it means that on the days when no one will drive me to a shop, I feel I have been a bit of a failure that day.

Taxi drivers are few and far between. In fact, there are only two in the whole Pewsey Vale and they shut up shop at 2am so there is difficulty getting back from parties.

We went to a party on top of our hill last summer. Because it was Covid, there had to be a limit of 30 people and the marquee had no sides – it was just a high awning on metal poles, carefully tethered with pointy bits dipping down, giving on to a panoramic view of the Pewsey Vale.

We warned one of the young females who was staying with us that, unless she left with us, she would be unable to get a taxi back. She declared that she would get a lift down with another guest named Sam.

Next day she told us that, at about 3am, when she saw that Sam was intent on 'doing the worm' until dawn, she decided to make her own way back but had not told anyone she was leaving as she didn't want to disrupt the party. Hence she had blithely walked – alone – along the dangerous A-road. It turned out she was more worried about cows in the fields than cars on the road.

Often we can ask benign-natured Derek, who lives in the village, to drive me to the station. But he is hard to get hold of since he is usually sitting on a mowing machine or wielding a power tool and cannot hear his phone ringing. However, he also delivers the newspapers in the morning and if I jump out and ambush him at that time he may be kind enough to drive me to the station. I mentioned this to a young guest who, needing to catch an early train, got the wrong end of the stick and pinned an imperious notice on the door, written in bold in a sharpie pen, commanding Derek to come at 7.15am to take *him* to the station.

As I opened the door to take the milk in I saw the notice in time to rip it down.

'That would have been a breach of etiquette,' I explained to our puzzled guest from London.

'Why?'

'Well, it would have been an invasion of Derek's privacy since other people driving past would have seen the notice and cottoned on that he sometimes gives us lifts.'

These are the sorts of things that take time for an urbanite to learn.

On one morning in July 2021, I looked out of the window when the door was knocked and there was my walking friend Carmen. She is a very smiley, all-good person who used to be our daily three times a week until sadly she had had enough of Giles, who followed her around wiping surfaces to see if there was still any dust. This caused Carmen to resign.

It was such a shame because my mother had been so pleased that I had found someone.

I can remember her exulting, 'Well that's marvellous. How many hours a day do you have her for?'

'Two,' I said.

'That's very good,' said my mother. 'Because if it was three you would have to give her a cup of tea.'

Carmen's husband was on the bins and they used to go to collect cans from Tidworth army camp. There were unopened cans dumped in abundance there with the labels washed off by the rain but, on the grounds that all tinned food remains edible indefinitely, they used to just eat their way through it, not knowing what it was but feeling confident they would not get food poisoning.

Carmen took me to the station and it was therapeutic just being with someone who is very content with her life. Carmen, whether by the nature of the sunny character she was born with or by natural philosophy, knows what she likes, which is cleaning and doing it well, looking after her family and their dogs, and going on a caravan holiday twice a year. She's a breath of fresh, unpretentious air. It is of course possible to walk to the station but it takes an hour.

One day I had to walk to a local artist's house, which was only one mile away, but how would I transport the giant roll of bubble wrap which I had promised to deliver? Lucian, my junior assistant at the time, had a brainwave and brilliantly fashioned straps out of old tights. I wore the lightweight but unwieldy roll on my back like a rucksack. This is the sort of life hack that the young have learned from going to pop festivals.

Tensions with Strimming and Fruit

MARY:

We have moved the table of Room 4 into the window. It means only four people can sit at it, but we can look out at the foliage and the dew and waving cow parsley and, of course, it only reminds me that Stu will come with his strimmer any day now and do his herbicide, and Giles will freak out.

Things being cut down has always been a 'trigger' for Giles. And it runs in the family. Giles's Uncle Alan spent most of his adult life in a psychiatric hospital following a breakdown during National Service. Apparently schizophrenia was triggered when he was working for something like the Forestry Commission, and he tried to replant a lot of trees that had been cut down.

These days of course Uncle Alan would have been diagnosed as suffering from PTSD as both his parents had died. In fact, he was orphaned by 17 and his 27-year-old stepmother took over his childhood home, sending him into lodgings. Today he would have had years of therapy and not been locked up.

Funnily enough, having known Giles for 40 years, I only found out two weeks ago that he had a secondary reason for hating to see vegetation being trimmed down.

It might never have come up had I not asked him the following question:

'I know your mother has always been a keen gardener. But I have never known whether Godfrey was a keen gardener too?'

Giles replied, 'My mother used to have a very romantic type of garden with bowers, where plants and shrubs would be allowed to spill over on to paths in a naturalistic manner, but my father's main interest in the garden had been his enjoyment of using a strimmer. Often my mother would find that her efforts had been spoiled because my father had come along and tidied up the trailing tendrils of climbing roses, etc., and strimmed everything back to within an inch of its life.'

Clearly this was upsetting – traumatising even to me

just to hear about it – and it partly explains his phobia of Stu strimming the cow parsley on the bank opposite the cottage. When I pointed this out to Giles he replied, 'Oh. You are clever. I hadn't made that connection, Mary.'

On a similar theme, as a child Giles was programmed to eat fruit each time the family set out on a car journey – it means that, even today, he always looks first for his car keys and then for a piece of fruit, each time he sets out on a car journey.

Hence if he goes out eight times in a day he will eat eight pieces of fruit in the car. He cannot seem to change that brain setting. The result is that while he associates setting out on car journeys with eating fruit, I associate them with having rushes of cortisol going through my own system if I am his passenger, because I think, well if he can't change that illogical brain setting, then he will be unable to change any other brain settings such as the tendency to annoy neighbours, which is a homage to his father who made a speciality of this.

Walking and Talking

MARY:

Dr Michael Mosley on the radio has made a case for it being better for walkers to go first thing in the morning because there is something about the light at that time that triggers your brain into getting going.

Unfortunately it doesn't suit me to go out first thing in the morning as that is the time when my brain works best so I need to be working at my desk. However, Sarah from the next village goes past every morning at about 10am and sometimes she knocks to see if I want to join her walking around the block with her Labradors.

Ambulare solvare. When you walk you solve problems. It's to do with talking at great length – your primary objective is the exercise so you don't think too much about what you are saying and the unrestrained babbling can be productive. Moreover, as I never tire of pointing out, you are not making eye contact with your fellow walker and in that way the experience replicates the psychiatrist's couch.

One day Sarah and I picked up Penny, who lives a mile away. During the two-mile walk it emerged that Penny's husband had got himself into a state about whether or not he might have prostate cancer but had refused to go to the doctor for a PSA test. Instead, he had become super grumpy, wouldn't go out to social events and asked Penny not to have people in. Penny was in tears until I told her my plan of action. The husband didn't know my voice so I rang the landline (while he was in the garden – Penny tipped me off that he was not inside) and left a message on the answerphone claiming to be ringing from the surgery and asking him to book in for a 'routine PSA test'. It worked a treat. Men – to stereotype them – don't like initiating appointments with doctors but are delighted to cooperate if summoned for a 'routine' test.

Ambulare solvare.

On another day, when community-minded Sarah was bagging up beer cans tossed into the hedge, a woman called Magda drove by at speed, almost knocking Sarah into the now cavernous verge – a lot of these have been gouged out by reversing Amazon delivery drivers – creating a series of pitfalls into which cyclists like our carpenter Patrick have tumbled when making way for the van drivers. Patrick broke his collarbone.

Magda saw Sarah's outraged face in her car mirror and reversed at speed to ask did she have a problem.

'Well, you were driving bloody fast,' replied Sarah. 'And yes, I have to admit that I walk here every day and everyone who passes in a car is always really friendly, slows down to make sure my dogs are OK, and you are the only one who just drives past looking angry and not waving or smiling.'

She expected Magda, to whom she had never spoken before, to tear a strip off her. Instead Magda looked sad. She explained that she had too much on her plate. She spent all day driving between her ailing mother and picking up children from two different schools as well as working part-time. It became clear to both of them that this encounter had brought a sort of epiphany to Magda. And now she realised that her driving speed was a cry for help. It said look at me. I have to drive at this speed because I have too much to do. As a result of this realisation Magda stopped driving so fast and always looks much cheerier now when she purrs past us at a reasonable country-lane speed.

During lockdown, I sometimes used to wait for Sarah on a wall outside Patsy's house. Patsy would look out of an upper window and talk to me. I would talk about how I was averaging 15,000 steps per day but had not lost any weight. She would talk about how she swam 32 lengths each day but had not lost any weight either. I had never spoken to her before lockdown. How would I ever have had the opportunity?

When I lived in Wellington Square, Chelsea, in the 1970s we didn't know any of our neighbours until the Queen's Silver Jubilee in 1977. Then we met them in the square garden and I remember feeling so much happier as I went to sleep on subsequent nights, picturing the other square residents – now that I knew them – settling down into their own bedrooms. It was suddenly like being at a boarding school, rather than in an alien pod, and made all the difference to a sense of cosiness.

How do Giles and I fit into the countryside in a social context? Well, it might have been different in the past if we were moving in, as strangers into an already closed community, as for example might have been the case if you moved into a Devon village in the 1960s and before the M4 was built. It wasn't that people would be unfriendly, but just that everyone would have already had their social life sorted with people with shared histories and backgrounds.

Now I think that not only have we been here long enough for others locally not to see us as entirely unre-latable, especially since Clap for Carers during lockdown and undertaking more shopping for each other, but also we incomers are now probably almost a third of the local population.

Before the Brexit vote, David Goodhart identified the two tribes that live in Britain today: the Anywheres, the well-travelled people who take a more international view of life who can feel at home virtually anywhere; then there are the Somewheres, who feel a deep identification with their home territory and do not want to leave it or have it invaded by outsiders. They will only feel happy in their ancient territory. I posit that Giles and I are a cross between the two tribes. I myself still feel like a radio not fully tuned because I am no longer surrounded by Northern Irish people. Giles longs for the Shropshire Hills, the Long Mynd and the small fields. The Somewheres and Anywheres are also analogous to the 'Virtuals' – those who conduct most of their business lives online – and the 'Physicals' who do the real-life work – the gardeners, the bin people, the taxi drivers, the doctors and nurses and the teachers.

Some of my happiest interactions have been with 'Somewheres' such as local men Denis the rat catcher and Kevin the plasterer. Denis has told me that he and his Jack Russell have been happy every day of their lives 'doing what needs doing'. Kevin, who always wears shorts, even in winter, and stretches a lot with his arms above his head so you can see his taut torso, finds plastering work enjoyable, 'because you can see the progress you have made at the end of the day'. Kevin walked 100 miles along the Jurassic Coast last summer in order to raise money for a charity. He averages four miles an hour.

Then there's Martin, who drives a septic-tank-empty-ing lorry with a logo saying 'No jobbie too big' on its side. He has been emptying septic tanks his whole working life 'and I wouldn't change a day of it'. He comes twice a year and chats with us as the squelching goes on. He told me that one of his other clients, a cancer specialist, was against the competent (i.e. fully leak-proof) septic tank. He thought the microscopic amounts of escaping fluids, which filtered their way back into the water supply, were an important factor in immunosuppression and that 'a little bit of dirt in their water' was good for human beings. An interesting theory I had not heard expressed before.

AMARYL-
LIS AT THE
FAIR
RICHARD
JEFFERIES

BOOK COVER FROM 1908 – DUCKWORTH AND COMPANY

Village Testimonies

Richard Giles, Aged 75

Family and Childhood

Mother was from Pewsey. I have got nine volumes upstairs that I have put together of family history and I have found family people with origins in all the villages around. I've found and traced one family name 'Stone' in the Burbage records back 400 or 500 years. My father's family has been in Warminster certainly for 500 years. Oh yes, I'm a Wiltshire Moonraker.

I was born in Pewsey in what was then called West End. My father was a railwayman so he was a railwayman all over the place. He was down in South Wales as a young man where he was a signalman. He was at Pewsey for 25 years and then down at Patney and Chirton junction, which was the branch line off to Devizes. That was a big signal box. It was busy with the direct traffic to the west of England.

Growing up we children were very much close to nature, I suppose. A lot of spare time was spent playing out in woods going for long, long walks. Going gathering stuff like chestnuts, hazelnuts, mushrooms, watercress, blackberries, all that kind of stuff. We went for a walk every Sunday and we always got mother a bunch of wild flowers if they were available so you knew where to get the sweet-scented violets and primroses and cowslips.

Father had a veg-growing patch and another one at mother's mother, who lived at the other side of Pewsey at Dursden Lane. I was introduced to that very early because at the age of eight my father said to me, 'You're not getting any pocket money but I will cut up this wood,' which was sleepers, 'and you split it and tie the sticks in bundles and you can hawk them round Pewsey in a two-wheeled handcart to certain customers who would use it for kindling.' Then they would pay me four pence per bundle. I had plenty of money.

What Local Shops There Used to Be

I suppose I spent that money on sweets and things. We were coming out of the rationing and I remember it was about four ounces of sweets a week, which we had delivered by our grocer every Thursday night. Our grocer was Les Baker who had a shop located at the top of Dursden Lane right on Milton Road. That was a shop there. His brother had a chimney sweep business who also lived there, and both of them lived there with their mother.

I went away for a bit to study and when I came back I became aware of the decline in the number of bakers – because there were about five bakers in Pewsey, then we had a decline in butchers, because we had three butchers' shops, and a fishmonger, well he was a butcher and fishmonger, opposite the Moonrakers pub.

If you had some special event and you wanted to hire some formal attire, Moss Bros or something like that, you'd go into Nichol's – they'd phone London, it would be put on the train and be down that evening. It was pretty good. Jane Nichol's father, he used to have to get on his bike and deliver something like that, up to Everleigh or something. Most of the tradesmen had vans; you had milk, bread, meat, coal delivered. There would also be a tallyman.

A tallyman would come round, probably from a tailor or shoe dealer, where you would pay so much a week and you'd probably build up a credit, so you could have a brand-new pair of shoes. But people were a bit prudent like that because many of them belonged to Christmas clubs based in the local pub. You'd pay sixpence or a shilling a week, then at Christmas they'd all pay out and there you'd have the extra money to spend.

The Changes in Farming

I have noticed the great decline in dairy farming. There are a few large dairy herds but there used to be dairy herds all over the place. When we were children, milk was put in churns and collected by tanker. The stillages were at the side of the road so the milk lorry could draw up alongside and just rotate the churns across into the back.

We were aware that fields were getting bigger but that had happened before with steam ploughing. I remember as a youngster, Woodborough nurseries, they had extensive fields of daffodils and tulips, and large numbers of ladies were seasonally employed to pick and they would be put into hampers and go up to Woodborough or Pewsey railway station. Taken off to market. It's a bit like the watercress, which operated at Milkhouse Water, and lots of satellite watercress beds about that would all be gathered in and packed into chip baskets and put on the goods trolleys on the railway station platform and they would go to London and on to the Midlands markets. There's loads of stuff used to go from Pewsey, agricultural stuff, north of the railway station. I do remember as a youngster every so many years a gang would be sent from Cooper's in Oxford to dig up horseradish. They'd dig it up to make horseradish sauce. You've got to let it re-establish. And there used to be apple orchards up at Oare, Oscar Peel. I don't know much about how they were marketed.

See, the soil in the Vale of Pewsey is largely based on upper greensand now that makes a fairly friable agricultural soil. It's not quite as good as the lower greensand, which is larger particle size. You get that at Bromham, which is quite a market garden area. It's sandy here but you can rub it to dust.

I feel a sadness looking back on how life used to be, principally, I suppose, because of not exactly a decline of agriculture but of a change in agriculture. Go back 100 years and villages like Charlton would have had loads of people working on the farms. I am interested in conservation but a lot of people who get into it are like religious extremists; they only see their point of view and that's got to be pursued at all costs.

Changes in Village Social Life

All the small villages would have had big populations. I was looking at a book of old postcards of the Vale and pictures of the village schools had 50, 60 children in, so there was a big population that made a great difference socially.

Now if you take the older men ... where did they go in the evening? They had no television, they went to the local pub. They played darts and dominoes and crib and stuff like that, and they had a few beers and gossips and perhaps a bit of singing. They were far, far more sociable than people are today. That's the thing that has declined sharply.

The advent of phones, people walking about with their faces buried in those little keypads, not listening to anybody else. The thing that we have lost which I remember well: when I first started going to licensed premises 60 years ago, if you wanted to discuss something, to buy something, you just went to the pub. You would ask other people for their experiences. You could get advice like that, if you wanted help on a project: go down the pub on a Saturday night and you'd have a ton of volunteers.

I know a lot of things are better but some things are not and certainly the sociability has been hit. Most villages had a football team, lots of villages in the Pewsey Vale had a band, a brass band or a silver band, all kinds of things like that.

We haven't got a WI any more. We haven't got an Evergreen Club for the elderly. We don't have dart leagues. There's no push-ball team in Pewsey any more. The emergence of these horrid fences, which make houses look like fortresses ...

Privacy Privacy Privacy

This is the era of the six-foot-high close-boarded fence. Privacy has become a mania. When I was a youngster, people around their garden might have a three-foot-high hedge that kept the animals out of the garden but you could stand behind your hedge and talk to your neighbour walking down the street. Now these fences ... I'm surprised they haven't got barbed wire on the top of them. Ooh, I have seen those things going up everywhere; people spend thousands of pounds on this privacy. They have vast, high things. Hedges seem to be vastly higher than they used to be, and they cost far more to maintain.

Today people don't know each other as well. There are a number of reasons for that. People don't talk to each other as much. This obsession with privacy and fences and stuff. People don't go out and socialise as much. The proportion of people who go to the local pub has really gone down but I suppose those going to coffee shops has gone up a bit. It's a complex picture.

Is Anything Better?

I suppose you could say communication is better today than it was in the past, but in the old days people communicated with postcards and they would be delivered within 24 hours and there was more than one delivery a day.

Chris Wootton, Aged 69, Shopkeeper

I was born in Beechingstoke. My family is all in the churchyard now. Unfortunately the younger family members have obviously been priced out of the housing market – they have had to spread their wings further afield.

But I went to Woodborough School and then on to Devizes Grammar. I went straight to work at T.H. White [outdoor goods supplier]. I wasn't a school lover. It was easy to walk into a job, the year I left school. There were five full pages of adverts in the *Gazette & Herald* every week – five full pages!

I worked here first in 1978, then I took it on from my old boss in 1987. We were agricultural engineers to start with then they progressed into the retail world and then my old boss just lost interest in it and said to me one day, 'Do you want to take it on?' And the rest is history.

I've seen my customers change a lot – oh yeah! The older generation is far more loyal than the younger generation. They've been brought up with internet shopping. They don't really know too much about local shops, do they? Everything is online and its Amazon this and Amazon that. People come in saying, 'I could get that cheaper online.' Or they say, 'I want so and so because I have been let down by my online delivery,' and that really frustrates me, I tell you.

But we have a much wider range of stock now whereas before there was a lot of garden machinery and most of my customers are very appreciative of what I do.

We do get told occasionally, 'Oh, you can't get anything in Pewsey,' and we have to remind them we are not a big town, we are not a big city. In Pewsey in general you haven't got a bad range of shops, although when I first started we had three banks, two building societies and a post office and now all we have got is a post office. And then Nichol's, that was a fantastic institution. It used to bring a lot of people into the village. Yes, there were three butchers, greengrocers, TV and radio, chemist, toy shop in the high street, bakers, the International Stores, a general grocery – they went in the late seventies.

Before Covid, and after the housing estate was built, we had a whole different set of faces on a Saturday than we had during the week. Commuters, you see. They built all the housing but no infrastructure improvements – you've still got one doctor's surgery and one school, yet they've tagged all these houses on.

Sometimes another shop springs up and then it's gone. Some of the blame is on the council and the government for that with business rates which are a big killer for places like Pewsey. You open up a business tomorrow, you pay the full business rate irrespective of how long it takes you to build up your business.

I've seen a lot of changes, oh God yeah. All the small farms have disappeared – there were lots of small farms when I started out. Some have gone where there's houses, others have been swallowed up by farming corporations. I mean, Mr Wookey at Upavon was a good customer. He used to have three combines on each farm – he had Rushall farm and Upavon farm. Now you're lucky if you have one big combine to service God knows how many farms.

Pewsey is not in a good state, because two big things have affected footfall in our shop and they all happened within months of each other. Firstly, when the council shut the tip and the recycling centre and, secondly, when Lloyds Bank shut, so people have had to go out of Pewsey to go to the tip and they've got to go out of Pewsey to do their banking and, of course, when they're out of Pewsey in Marlborough or Devizes they're going to do their other things, especially with the cost of fuel.

I was lucky I got on the property ladder just when they were building Heron Homes up there. As soon as that was built, prices rocketed because of the commuter belt, so that's had a very negative effect.

When I look back at my childhood and how Pewsey is now, I would sum it all up like this: change, change, change, and not necessarily for the better.

Sara Tiplady, Aged 60, from Ramsbury

Escaping to the Country After Life in Cities

I know what it's like to live in a city. When I was 18, I went straight from here in Ramsbury and an all-girls boarding school, and I trained as a nurse in Whitechapel. In my third year I lived in Poplar in east London on the 11th floor of a tower block. It was a concrete jungle and you didn't dare use the lifts because they were full of druggies and alcoholics – although mostly unconscious.

After my really sheltered background it was brilliant for me because it really opened my eyes to what else is out there.

I met and married a doctor and we moved around every time he got a new job, which was about every two years. We lived in Islington and we lived in Oxford.

And then my mum passed away in 2007 and I came back to Ramsbury to help my dad. My children were growing up by this point and I had got divorced sadly.

I wouldn't want to live in a busy town again. I really like the pace of life in the country and I love being outside, which is why I set up my dog-walking business and I know every dog in Ramsbury. Even if somebody gave me a flat in London or in Leamington Spa I wouldn't want to leave here. I even try to never go to Swindon. It used to have a small town feel to it, but no longer.

Returning to Roots and to a Village Lifestyle

My dad was the GP here since 1961. Ramsbury was always a wonderful community, and it still has that community feel about it even though we now have around 2,000 people. There are families who have been here for generations and generations, but now there are more people moving down here from London – you can still get to London in an hour. There are a few second homes and there's an estate on the outskirts with about 65 houses. They're trying to get more planning through for building but thankfully it's a conservation area, so they can't do much in case they spoil the countryside. The new-build houses have attracted younger families, because the school's good. That's certainly something that's changed: the school wasn't any good when I was young.

Why Ramsbury Is the Ideal Village

Most significantly, Ramsbury still has shops. These little shops are an absolute lifeline for people. Literally, because we live in a valley and sometimes in heavy snow it's almost impossible to get out! The grapevine in Ramsbury is very active. Say someone came to Ramsbury as a complete outsider, as soon as somebody in the village knows you're moving in there's a welcome pack that goes out with all the information about clubs, societies, library opening times, shops, the tennis courts, the cricket, the football, etc.

We even have am dram – we have the Ramsbury Players who are just brilliant. They put on about two productions a year. The plays are written by local villagers, and performed by them too. There's the Roxy, the cinema, it's where we project films like any cinema, all the ones that have just come out, and it's only £4 a seat.

There are driving forces behind that. There's the parish council which is very active. There's Ian Smith, who is very much a focal point for anything in the village. And Sheila Glass, who is the chair of the council. He's Mr Ramsbury, and she's Mrs Ramsbury. If you want to know anything, it's them you go to. Then of course there's the women in the post office – they know everyone and everything about everyone. I suppose I'm also one of those people. It's not possible to run a village dog-walking business and not know about what's going on in the village.

This village has a certain sense of continuity. When my house came on the market I didn't even go to see it, I just bought it. My side of the High Street is just gold dust – the gardens go down to the River Kennet. I knew I had to snap it up immediately.

With Ramsbury you have the sort of village where the more you put in the more you get out of it. There are plenty of opportunities to volunteer and get stuck in with the community, and you'll find it very rewarding. But then if you also want to move here and live quietly, that's your choice and people respect that. If you go into a shop and you're asked how you are and you say you're fine, no one's going to dig any deeper than that. But equally everyone knows that if you do want to share what's going on, your husband's ill, your son's unhappy at school, etc., whether with a shopkeeper or a neighbour, what have you, people are glad to listen.

And we don't really have crime, not really.

Romantic Life in the Village

There are lots of single women in their sixties who are all quite happy on their own, but if they wanted to find a new partner I think it would be easier to find one here than in London. You're more likely to find people who are like-minded and have similar interests, in the clubs, societies, etc. in the village, which are always well attended. For example, the bowls club – people tend to be of the same age and interests. We manage to organise bus trips and all sorts so that we can have competitions with villages and towns across Wiltshire. If you go on a dating app everything has to happen really quickly or not at all, but it does seem that, in Ramsbury, you can build up relationships with people in a more traditional, slow and stress-free fashion.

The elderly in the village have carers. They are very well known and get booked out very often. Then there are the agency workers who you'll see walking around in their purple uniforms. That's something I've done in the past, I've done private care because I used to be a nurse so I can. The surgery we have here as well is fantastic. That's another great thing about this village. It's really well known. They really look after you, and more often than not you can get an appointment on the day.

It seems to be that much of the good in Ramsbury is to do with the personalities involved. You're very lucky that you've got public-spirited people. I mean, a lot of the good in this village works through volunteers; for example, the charity shop raises a huge amount of money for projects in the village – the bowls club alone gets about £500 every two months or so, purely from the charity shop. Well, the main cost we have is the cost of maintaining the green. We mow it every other day, but then the fertilisers etc. cost several thousand a year. Then of course the electricity, etc. There is a membership fee which is £95 a year, and we play from April to October. We've got about 30 members at the moment. Then there are the social members who pay £20 a year just to come up and have a drink, a cup of tea, but they don't play.

Andy Martin, Aged 72, Fencer, Tree Feller

Working Life

I was born in Devizes, left school at 15 and got work on a farm. From the age of 12 you would go to Stan Taylor, a farmer in Woodborough, and he would let you drive the tractor and do a bit of rolling or chain harrowing. As soon as you could push a clutch in, you would be on the bale cart.

Then you would go to Rodney Smith and he would let you do a bit more, then Alan Latham would let you do even more. So as the older boys left the farm into a proper job, you'd move, you'd change farms – so by the time you actually got to get a proper job you had probably worked three or four years at least with men, doing a man's job, so by the time you were 16 you had a good idea of what work was.

And then I got offered work at Keevil airfield in a grass dryer. My father's best friend, he offered me a job down there – so I went down there at 16 and we were on 12-hour night shifts and there were two men on each shift. I was a man and I got paid exactly the same as the next man who could have been 45 and had four kids, and we split the money four ways. So I earned a lot of money that season and then, when they started to lay, cos it's generally seasonal work, I was told I could stay on in the workshops but I said no – there are married blokes.

Mr Dunford had mentioned this job at the sawmill so I said, 'Sooner go and let a married man have my place,' so I went to the sawmill where I stayed for quite a while.

Social Life and Gun Life as a Teenager

Well, we had youth clubs to start with. I mean when you're 11 years old we had Woodborough youth club, and then that was on Monday nights, and I think on Tuesday nights you'd go to Upavon youth club – if you knew the date you could just turn up at other people's youth clubs. You could go to youth clubs three or four nights a week if you wanted to.

But once you worked on the farm that was where most of your time went – that would be evenings during the summer and then in the winter you'd take a few rabbits ... shooting pigeons. I mean kiddy stuff stopped at 12. You went into more grown-up stuff.

When I had my oral examination for my CSE [Certificate of Secondary Education] at Pewsey, you had to pick a subject to talk about so I decided to talk about my guns. I took a 12-bore and a 0.410. I broke them down and wrapped them up and took them on the school bus, then put them in the headmaster's office. When we were doing the CSE I went up and took them from the headmaster, got them on the table, explained all about shotguns, waved them about a bit. Then I had to go back, put them back in his office, and after school I took them back on the school bus.

Well, you imagine a 15-year-old taking a brace of shotguns to school today but it was normal, it was absolutely normal because that's what everybody did.

Pub Life in the Villages in the Sixties

We used to work on a circuit on a Friday night – you'd go to your locals. You might start in the Prince of Wales in Hilcott, which is now a house, and then go up to the Seven Stars at Bottlesford, and then you'd have met up with some others and you might have thought you'd go to the Clock at Lydeway, or you might go to the Antelope at Upavon, then you might come and finish up at the Charlton Cat.

You might take in three or four pubs and you'd actually meet other mates of yours that are going the opposite route. You didn't stay about long. Drink driving wasn't about then as long as you could do a straight line but your driver didn't drink much. I mean, that's when pubs were for drinking not for eating. I think the Seven Stars, you got the choice of chicken in a basket or scampi in a basket with a handful of chips and that was it. It was just us – no wives or girlfriends.

Once I was married we used to go out to the Prince of Wales but we didn't go to the pubs like we used to. No, well, we had a family.

We miss the pub days. Well, you haven't got the landlords now, have you? I took the wife the other night. We went down [to Wilcot] and I think he said two phrases. I asked for a shandy and a lemonade and can I have a red wine and he just said, 'Is Merlot OK?' That's the only thing he said to me, then he said to me, 'That will be £10.70.' No conversation. I mean, your old landlord he'd have it – it was like going into your barber's – you know you'd come into a conversation and discuss all sorts of things. You'd discuss local stuff.

Everyone Worked Locally

In the mid-1950s, that's when the farms started to run the staff down. They got more machinery and bigger machinery but until then the majority of villagers worked on the farms. When I was pre-15, most of the people cycled to work or they got picked up in a works bus. The building companies would come round and pick up all the men. Chivers's, they'd have a bus that would pick up for Devizes, a lot of people worked up at RAF Upavon, but most people worked locally, and they'd cycle or they'd walk to work. We had the bakers – Strong's bakers at Woodborough, about six delivery men, plus your bakers – that employed a lot of people.

Or they worked in local little businesses, like up in Bottlesford you had R. Ford & Son, with the lorries, or the fertiliser dealers, they employed 20 people or more. Harry Fitchitt, the demolition bloke, he employed six or seven people and that was just a quarter-mile up one road.

When the Villages Changed

I suppose in the seventies most people moved out to get jobs in towns. There wasn't the jobs for the youngsters any more. If you were lucky, you got a job for a local building company so you could stay local, but most moved away and, if you wanted to get married and get a house ... well, that's when I got a job at Marlborough College because, not as much money as at the sawmill, where I was felling timber for about £5 per week more, but it came with a free house.

I went to the college doing a sort of menial job in comparison, but I had a free house and you were looked after, not that you didn't get looked after at the sawmill. It wasn't quite so exciting as cutting the timber.

And then outsiders started coming into the villages. It's obviously escalated over the years but it started with the 1970s. I suppose a lot of houses had a lot of old people. Most of the youngsters had moved on and moved out into council houses, probably in Devizes or somewhere, unless you wanted to work on the farm or in the building trade. There weren't houses to rent in the villages and their parents would stay there in their houses and die.

Relationships with Landowners

I've had a very good relationship with Stan Taylor, oh very good, and that has lasted a lifetime because you work with them, and I'm still good friends with Rodney Smith – he always rings me up if he wants something doing. Alan Latham, of course, like him or hate him, he was pretty loyal and he'd treat us well.

Farmers Today Compared to Farmers in the Past

Well, your farmers now don't employ. Now it's basically just families working farms, so it's a completely different ball game. All the profits go into the pot and outsiders don't get much of a look-in.

When farmers had six or seven men working, they had to look after six or seven families so it was a little bit more worker-friendly. Those farmers were proper farmers, overseeing those families. A lot of responsibility. In Wilsford, most of the houses were owned by the farmer and most of the people worked on the farm and he looked after them.

By this I mean you could go on as a boy and get promoted up through the ranks and finish as a head cowman, which was good money. They would always look after your house for you, keep it together and when you retired – at 75 because you didn't retire at 65 – when you found you couldn't milk cows any more or manage tractor driving ... you'd get a job down the farmhouse in the garden doing vegetables. You could keep working until you dropped.

Of course, expectations weren't quite like what they are now. I mean, we didn't expect to have six or eight weeks holiday. And certainly not go abroad. Sunday school used to give us a day down in Swanage – that was a serious outing. Now kids would laugh if you said you were going down to Swanage for the day. When expectations grow, you start to lose reality. Really, you don't appreciate what a pound is really worth. People think that it's just a normal thing now to have your two or three weeks in Benidorm or somewhere.

Changes in the Pewsey Vale in the Seventies and Eighties

People laugh at me but I think the worst thing to happen to the Pewsey Vale has been the railway station. If it wasn't for the station, house prices would be a darn sight cheaper and you wouldn't get the idiots chasing through the village. If they said Pewsey station was going to close, I think that would be quite a good thing. I know some of the commuters are customers of mine but I think that is the price you'd have to pay.

I don't know if the heart would come back into Pewsey or not – I think it's probably too far gone now. Very few people in Pewsey know what the original Pewsey was like – they're dying. Somebody once said, 'When an old person dies, a library closes and the information is lost,' and that's perfectly true and there are lots of characters in Pewsey – we lose them every year now. I mean, anyone over 70 – because anyone under 70 would struggle to know.

The View from the School Gate

You think how Pewsey has gone downhill. It was very close knit. I mean, all the teachers at the school knew the kids and they'd see the kids out socially and they'd know your parents. You couldn't get away with much because the network was there but now ... Woodborough school ... there are kids that get bussed in ... parents bring them in from right outside the catchment area.

I mean, when I was at Woodborough school, John Dunford, I think, was the furthest walker and he used to walk from Hilcott and he'd walk up to Bottlesford ... John had already walked half a mile. When we got to station corner, Beechingstoke would come along and there'd be another seven or eight joining up. Everybody would walk to school.

There were only ever two cars that went into the school. They were both teachers', Mrs Stanton and Miss Lloyd – their cars were allowed into the playground. There were no cars pulled up. When they shut Wilsford school we had Mrs Jeffreys used to come over and she'd bring the six kids to Woodborough – that's fair enough because Wilsford is a little bit out of the way [2.5 miles] for a five-year-old to walk.

Some of the parents you see now, they must have spent an hour putting their slap on. They're all dressed up like they're going somewhere special. They all rock up in their cars and it's quite a social event dropping their kids off … the kids are a minor part. Whereas before, you know, we'd just say goodbye to mother and we would walk out of the door and join the rest.

Loss of Habitat

It's getting a bit better than it used to be. I mean back in the fifties it was proper.

Over here they cleared a lot out because that was all ploughed with steam tackle. Stratton's were the exception because they were the biggest farmers and they did contract ploughing for other people as well as for their own farm. They had big steam ploughs, which would plough huge distances – you winched the ploughs across with a pair of engines. I remember two pairs of plough engines parked up at Burbage Wharf cos decent tractors had started to come in then, and they could plough more efficiently than steam. That was one of the worst things when machinery got bigger. Then farmers were paid to take hedges out in the sixties and seventies to make it more economical for farming.

Most people didn't go much on that because that was habitat gone. Because back then there were still rural people in the villages. I mean, nowadays people wouldn't know – if they looked over the hedge, they wouldn't know what they were looking at – but then anything that happened outside your window people took notice of and an interest in. I suppose farmers were hoping bigger fields would reflect in a better standard of living for farm workers, more wages. Now, of course, they're getting paid to put them back in again, once they realised all the topsoil blew off – went like a prairie.

At the time it was happening, the people who really knew that that was habitat gone were getting too old to do much about it. The people that were young enough should have known better really but they didn't appreciate what was happening. The change from rural communities to dormitory villages had already started to happen so a lot of people look over the hedges and don't appreciate what is going on.

I had to take a couple of guns on a shoot. I had to take them down across a field and over a little brook into a coppice and it had snowed the night before and these two professional well-to-do gentlemen were discussing train timetables and I said, 'Excuse me.' I said, 'You are in one of the nicest parts of the country on a glorious day. It's just snowed. You couldn't wish to be in a better place and here you are talking about train times.' I said, 'Well, I can tell you now, we've had a cock pheasant come through here, we've had deer pass,' and I showed them all the footprints. 'You want to soak in your surroundings a bit,' I said.

And they both agreed that they unfortunately didn't know what they were looking at and they had both lived in the countryside for probably 20 years – one owned a bit of land – and they didn't actually know what was in their back garden. And I'm thinking it's a lost cause really unless you have got any knowledge of the circle of life within the countryside ...

And all these people have got a big say in it, they all vote, but when it comes to rural things they've got no idea what they're voting for. But I don't think you can get it back to anything like how we'd like it to be. I don't think people have got time now.

What's Good About the 'New Days'

People that move into the area are so ignorant in country ways that it keeps us in business. Most of the jobs me and Jerry [his son] do would once have been done by the people themselves.

John Dunford, Aged 71, Farmer, Timber Merchant

Early Life

I was born in Devizes hospital and I was born out of wedlock into a sort of farming family really. All my uncles and me lived with our gran. I went to Woodborough school. It was basically primary and everyone walked to school or bicycled. I used to walk from Hilcott, which was over two miles, at five years old, no assistance whatever the weather. And you know there were so many people living in the village then and you knew everybody so there was no concern about you being unsafe, really.

As you got further up the road two more children would tag along in Bottlesford and up through Broad Street, you would always be picking up a few more, so there was a little gang. Then Pewsey opened a secondary modern in 1957 and so I went there and then we got picked up by the bus every morning at the top of the lane.

I had three and a half years at Pewsey school and I was 15 and three months when I left. I finished school on Friday and started work on Monday at a garage in the village in Hilcott. I worked there for two years, then I went to work at the sawmill in Honeystreet and that is where I sort of learned my trade.

The Sawmill and the Other Local Industries

The sawmill was owned in those days by a guy called Dennis Slade. The Slades owned all the property in Honeystreet, except for the Builders Wharf and the pub, up until about 1958. Then they had a big sale at Marlborough at the Bear hotel and all the property was sold off. You know, houses were being sold and a typical terraced house was £350, £500, £400 in 1958.

So the sawmill closed down for three years then Dennis Slade bought the yard on the south side of the canal and started operating as a sawmill again.

Meanwhile, the other side of the canal was bought by Mr Neal from London, who was like a rag merchant. They used to buy in rags, sort them, clean them and then cut them up and sell them to industry for wiping rags and cleaning machinery and all stuff like that. By 1971 they were employing 56 people there. Most of them were like local women in the village who wanted to top up their income.

Everybody in the village worked. They bicycled to work – it was just the time when families were starting to have a car. We didn't have a car until 1968, I think, when I bought my first car then father bought one; there were so many businesses in the three villages – Alton Barnes, Woodborough and North Newnton.

If you were to go down that road you would probably find there were 400 people employed in the villages. And now there's hardly anybody. The employers would have been the farms, the sawmill, the butchers, the bakery at Woodborough – it had five vans on the road delivering bread to the villages – you had Woodborough nurseries and a lot of women worked there to supplement their income, you had Woodborough station [pre-Beeching] with seven or eight people working, all the men repairing the lines, the gangers on the lines. In the 1950s, well the Jewish people would come, probably two or three with the hats and the hair. Because all the milk used to go into London from Woodborough station. So they used to come here and go around all the farms at Wilsford, because they obviously knew what farms their milk came from – and they would bless the farm and the milk so that everything was kosher. Because everything has to be kosher.

All these jobs, they've all disappeared.

That kind of village life, I don't think we could get back to. It's a different type of life today isn't it? We had two or three village shops and every day there was a delivery of fresh bread. Strong's on a Monday, Wednesday and Friday, and the Co-op van on Tuesday, Thursday and Saturday, so you had fresh bread every day.

And now people go to a supermarket and they fill the boot of the car up with cardboard boxes basically. But years ago you'd have one cardboard box with the ingredients in and everybody used to make their own stuff, so that's how things have changed. Now you go and fill the back of the car up but you haven't really got anything, it's all packaging.

The sawmill started in 1810 when the canal started. A guy called Henry Robbins, he had a little sawmill up by Woodborough church, and they must have seen potential when the [canal] opened and they moved to the wharf.

And he operated it for 40 years and then he went in with someone else and it was called Robbins and Pinniger and they traded for nearly 100 years up until 1958. And they were probably one of the biggest employers in the west of England in a rural setting. You had to go to Bristol to find anywhere bigger. They had wagon-making facilities, wheelwrights, tarpaulin makers, thatching spars, they were slate merchants, coal merchants and they made their own bone meal fertiliser, which they were quite famous for.

Nineteen fifty-eight they finished. And then I went off in the early 1970s and did my own thing, a bit of tree felling. And then it got taken over in 1978 by a big timber importer from South Wales and they thought they were going to mill their own timber and that, but they didn't have a clue and they got into difficulty by 1990, and that's when I bought it. I bought half in 1980, which I was using as a base. And sort of changed the whole perspective of how it operated.

I employed about seven but I just looked at it – you have to adapt.

I could see there were people moving into the area and they were not local. People were being made redundant off the farms who lived in farmhouses, and they'd move away. Then the farmhouse was sold and someone from London or elsewhere would buy it. Then they want to buy a bit of land off the farmer, well they needed two acres which needed fencing, so that's how I operated my business.

At the time we were lucky because, around the year 2000, there were so many TV programmes doing decking and that sort of thing, and that helped the business. Now it's all cooking programmes.

When I worked for the sawmill [when young] you didn't cut timber for any local people, it was all timber for British Steel for making pallets for coal mines for pit blocks. You were sort of doing jobs for all the big industries, you know. But that all went out of the window because British Steel fell apart. And I used to fell ash trees in Savernake for Slazenger. The tennis racquet people used to come and buy the trees and make the tennis racquets. Ercol furniture used to buy the elm for chair seats. All that has disappeared.

Handles, paint-brush handles. We are cutting up logs for firewood now that we would have died for years ago to make into these products.

We had all the skills in Honeystreet. Well, you can still see the quality. The sawmill built houses. You can see the Station Hotel down by the railway line – if you look at the quality of the brickwork and under the eaves it was all done to such a high standard, just because people had pride.

I don't know who taught them. It must all have been self-taught. You didn't go to college, you went to work for somebody and got an interest in it and that's what you did. You did that for life and you were good at it. That's how I learned most of my stuff. I haven't been to college – the only qualification I've got is a HGV licence. That's the only exam I've ever taken.

The population of Honeystreet has not changed much in the last 20 years because all the changes happened back in the eighties when the generation a bit older than me, when they lost all their jobs locally, they had to move to somewhere like Devizes and get a job for the council, for example, where they might have once had a job at the sawmill doing a skilled job. It's all changed so much.

And when they all move away then gradually the village dies; it's a gradual process. In Honeystreet, there's just one person who has been there for over 50 years. People used to have a job and work for somebody and they just stayed in that house for all their life. They wouldn't be moving around all over the place. The old girl who lived in Canal Cottage, which belonged to British Waterways, and her father worked on the canal. She was born there and she was 93 when she went – she'd been there for all that time. All those things have changed.

People buy and sell houses in places like Honeystreet and they are just so expensive for any younger people to be able to move in. I think all the changes started in the seventies and eighties. The supermarkets killed the local bakeries, then people started to travel round a bit more because they had a car, they'd go to Swindon shopping, to Tesco. When you start trying to analyse it, it's just a totally different lifestyle. And now with the internet you can get anything tomorrow. I can't be arsed with the technology.

We got to educate our kids differently. I left school when I was 15 and I was doing a man's job. Me and Andy Martin, we worked together, I was 19 and he was 17, felling trees, and we used to turn up to fell some beech trees somewhere. Well, if you had a 19- and 17-year-old turn up with a big timber tractor weighing 10 tonnes, with a tree overhanging a house and you put a winch on it, people would have a fit these days. But when we went out to work every day it was an adventure. We were invincible!

But now health and safety has killed everything. They just cut a tree down by the village hall – there were about eight blokes, they had a monster cherry picker and they were there for two days. Well, me and Andy would have gone there and done it in two hours.

National Service was a good thing in some respects. A lot of these people, carpenters, bricklayers, they all did National Service. It got them well disciplined to be able to work on their own account. It got them out of the village.

STANDING DEAD WOOD FOR OVERWINTERING INVERTEBRATES

Section 8

VILLAGE POLITICS

On community politics, beleaguered
Arcadia and trespassing

GILES:

A fair number of middle-class folk will throw themselves into local conservation, saving this or that common from development or local wetlands from being drained. Or they may become interested in parish-pump politics and may even become parish councillors.

The power of this lowest rung on the ladder of our democracy seems to be haemorrhaging recently due to the general tendency towards centralisation. Do parish councillors really count? Serving as a parish councillor does not appeal to me or my wife because so many rustic problems are of a mind-numbingly boring nature revolving around septic tanks or intractable quarrels about boundaries, fences and rights of way. I also think that local policies face an uphill struggle against a government intent on riding roughshod over the concerns of local hobbits. There is also the fear that if you give little people too much power it might encourage local corruption — allowing bribery to take place.

Pitfalls and Planning Horrors

GILES:

One of the most attractive prospects of voting in a Labour government is that the bank accounts of planning officers should be available for scrutiny under the Freedom of Information Act. However, a friend in the know tells me that bribers often get around this by gifting the planning officer an expensive new BMW rather than paying cash into their account – allegedly.

Whatever the scenery, some people move to the country only to find that a mushroom factory opens next door with all its concomitant weird smells and emissions of toxic vapours.

Intensive chicken factories can also cause olfactory offence if they decide to open up in a field near you. And your quality of life in the country might be governed by whether your local pub has remained open or has become extinct along with your bus service and poor broadband, which means you cannot work from home.

MARY:

Our own local pub – which was the heart of the community in many ways – had to close because the landlord wanted to sell it. Two benign local magnates considered buying it until they were advised that no pub will make a profit any more unless it reinvents itself as a gastropub. The premises were simply too small for this and so it lies mournfully unused, while the owner tries to get planning permission for it to become a house and all of those who previously laughed there have to walk wistfully by each day knowing this source of welcome is no longer there for them – a bit like having a dead parent.

GILES:
Some of the most trying issues for rural incomers of a sensitive nature like myself fall into the category which used to be called First World Problems, although I think that phrase has now been cancelled. These include purple trees and shrubs, and the smell of other people's barbecues. I approve of cockerels crowing and church bells ringing.

The wife and I have noticed a decoration trend in the houses of nouveau riche people. This is to make the interiors of their houses look like hotels, and the gardens and grounds also conform to the landscape gardens of five-star hotels, i.e. no trip hazards, plenty of concrete, defined flower beds and everything mown to within an inch of its life. So anything that grows must be within rectangular units surrounded by railway sleepers and nothing must be allowed to interfere with the mown sward, which has to be accessible to a sit-on mower. This trend to improve and tidy the landscape must have been going on for many decades as a book I inherited from my mother's library, *Through the Woods* by H.E. Bates, written in 1936, refers to his dislike of 'prim' fields in the new, clean-shaven landscape, no doubt aided by an arsenal of chemical weedkillers.

Villagers tinkering with abandoned or broken vehicles all day in the road – 'down from townies' don't like that.

The worst offence of all is to install wind chimes, which probably originate in a country where the wind rarely causes them to chime, but as increasingly squally and blustery weather patterns cause these musical instruments to become a cacophony, they can only be a form of torture to those hapless neighbours within earshot and who resent this incursion into traditional British culture.

Finally, the problem that outweighs all of these in Arcadia is the unfortunate modern habit of feeding the birds from bird feeders, which will only result in there being fewer songbirds. These feeding stations are, in effect, helpful to raptors higher up the food chain who use them as a takeaway service, i.e. sparrowhawks snatching blue tits drawn to the vicinity. They have also resulted in Richard Jefferies' favourite bird, the greenfinch, becoming almost extinct in this country as a result of a disease it picks up from poor hygiene at such feeding stations.

Trespassing and Rights of Way

GILES:

I will outline the background to my own recent crime incident.

Butterflies of conservation concern are making a welcome comeback — particularly on farmland where stewardship schemes, such as the non-persecution of thistles, can deliver entry-level improvements for insects.

The clouded yellow does not always fly in a straight line so, to get a good photograph with my newfangled iPhone in my capacity as self-elected biodiversity recorder, I entered a field, no more than a couple of hundred yards from the cottage, and was walking harmlessly along a tramline when I heard the sound of a quad bike roaring along the side of the field.

'Who's there?' bawled the familiar voice of Stu Varden, who works for the Big House. 'You're trespassing!'

I was wearing a small straw hat bearing the legend 'Croatia' and, assuming Stu, who has lived within 100 yards of us for 30 years, had failed to recognise me, I doffed the hat and called, 'It's only me, Stu. Your neighbour, Giles.'

'Makes no difference who it is. You're still trespassing. Come out of there now.'

I began to explain that post-Brexit agricultural enviro-schemes under Michael Gove envision a new era of cooperation where conservationists and landowners will wander hand in hand, as it were, in a brave new world of an as yet unspecified grand unified agricultural theory of everything. In anticipation of that time, I was making a start by recording the biodiversity within the crop itself, rather than in the set-aside strip, as this would clearly be of relevance when establishing new guidelines.

'You're still trespassing,' Stu growled. 'Come out of there now.' He dismounted from his quad bike and began moving towards me.

'And if you talk any more rubbish,' shouted his uncle Jake Varden from the sidelines, 'you'll feel the sharp side of my fist.'

Unlike Dustin Hoffman in the celebrated *Straw Dogs,* the morality tale of what happens when a sophisticated townie comes face to face with the pure muscle power of the indigenae, I did not rise to the challenge. Because of financial cuts, Wiltshire Council can no longer afford the evening classes it once ran where the gentleman insect obsessive might learn the rudiments of self defence.

It is easy to explain this passionate episode as a desire not to lose face once Stu had realised I was not a common or garden trespasser. Most villages have been ethnically cleansed of their original tribes while ours hasn't yet. The Vardens have a strong territorial instinct based on blood ties, shared grievances, the extirpation of manual labour by machines and yuppie incomers. Then there is the epigenetic impulse to react in the way one might in the days when the appearance of a stranger could signal a threat to scarce resources.

I was naturally humiliated by my enforced retreat but Mary was unsympathetic. 'You like lawlessness and knuckle fighting when it's in *Poldark* but not so much in real life?'

'How would this have been resolved in *Poldark*?'

'Well, in Poldark's time it could have been resolved by some friendly drinks in the local ale house but they're all closed now.'

As a landowner with a public footpath bisecting my one-acre plantation I have certain privileges tempered by onerous responsibilities. To keep the path ship-shape and accessible to a certain prescribed width not exceeding two wheelchairs. To deal with overhanging foliage in a proactive manner and not to obstruct the footpath. In the interests of rewilding, to replicate a natural cataclysmic event for the provision of 'natural capital', namely the resource of dead wood to encourage invertebrates, fungi and woodpeckers, notably the extremely scarce lesser spotted variety. As a responsible steward of the environment I have mitigated the misdemeanour by advertising the obstruction of a fallen tree with a large yellow exclamation mark pinned to the tree trunk. Ramblers are 'invited' to take a short detour around the offence. But to my annoyance, I have noticed ramblers pausing, pointing at other coppicing work, and in some extreme cases taking photographs as evidence and gesticulating to their companions, churlish actions which have unsettled me.

Accordingly I am working on a notice to encourage ramblers to keep moving by resorting to the unfashionable injunction 'NO LOITERING', followed by a circular arrow diagram suggesting onward movement. It's only a matter of time now before the 'rights of way' officer knocks on my door. Of course, the key to making progress through the maze of complexities surrounding this issue is common-sense dialogue. I will waste no time in averring that ramblers are a breed apart: they are walkers with a political agenda in their rucksacks to find fault with landowners. Tell-tale signs of the species include mandatory ski sticks designed for scree walking in the Dolomites, and Ordnance Survey maps in transparent sleeves usually worn at great inconvenience to the map reader round the neck. Genuine walkers often go out ill-prepared for the sudden squalls occasioned by anthropogenic climate change and can be distinguished by wearing baggy jumpers, wellingtons and even ill-fitting brogues.

MARY:

Giles's gardening addiction has ruled out weekend lunch appointments for many years. He simply 'can't give the day up'. The non-gardeners who will be present at the lunch are disappointed but also baffled – 'Couldn't he have done the gardening on another day – rather like we all work during weekdays and then relax at the weekends?'

But Giles wants to garden every day.

GILES:

Mary, of course, is socially aspirational and longs to attend these lunches but if I see the sun going down behind the clipped yew hedges of the secluded mansions, I cannot help but think of the final lines of Wilfred Owen's poem 'Futility':

> *Was it for this the clay grew tall?*
> *– O what made fatuous sunbeams toil*
> *To break earth's sleep at all?*

**A RARE VISITOR TO MY GARDEN – A LONG-EARED
OWL IN THE SCOTS PINE I PLANTED**

Section 9

ADDICTION TO GARDENING

On addiction, the philosophy of the twisted marshy morass and getting lost in the garden

Return to Nature

GILES:

You might not have heard of 31-year-old Joe Sugg. But to British millennials and members of Gen Z, he is ThatcherJoe – prankster and music maker. His YouTube channel, which launched in in 2012, is followed by 7.5 million people.

Or perhaps you caught him on the 2018 series of *Strictly Come Dancing*. According to a Sunday broadsheet, behind the jolly excitable boy-next-door persona, addicted to smartphones and the online world, lay a sensitive soul heading towards the buffers. 'I experienced social media burn-out,' Sugg admitted. Constantly comparing himself with others, he felt increasingly self-conscious and exposed.

Surprise, surprise, he turned to gardening during lockdown. Like many others, he fell into the Garden of Eden trap, and after lockdown could not get out of it again when Grant Shapps urged Britons to get back into their offices. In this three-page puff piece that I, as a minor TV celebrity, would kill for, it emerges that he has written a book.

Grow is part memoir, part lifestyle guide and also an entry-level gardening primer, designed to encourage other young people to reconnect with the natural world.

Gardening has long been a refuge for those in search of therapeutic physical cures. I mustn't mock the tendency of younger men to share their mental health issues rather than bottling them up as was the British norm under the banner 'Stiff Upper Lip', which has served me, royalty (except Prince Harry) and the officer class well for so many years.

When I was growing up, gardening still had the reputation, along with woodwork, as a useful remedial activity to which people such as burned-out businessmen could retreat. Monty Don made it sexy and the Prince of Wales showed us how ecological concerns through gardening for wildlife could help stem catastrophic biodiversity loss and, at the same time, sequester carbon for climate change mitigation.

Yet the question remains, 'But what does Giles do all day in the garden?' This asked Lord Mandelson of Mary when he came into the garden one afternoon with some mutual writer friends and surveyed the disarray. I was in Anglesey at the time.

'I don't know,' said Mary. 'But I do know he's in there all day long and comes back into the cottage exhausted each evening. I think he says he is making habitat for overwintering invertebrates.'

The book that changed my philosophy regarding gardening was purchased at Machynlleth's Centre for Alternative Technology in Wales. It is called *The Natural Garden Book: Gardening in Harmony with Nature* by Peter Harper, published in 1994. It was an iconoclastic book. I read with pleasure the heading 'Relinquish Control' – the advice therein consists of simply not doing things. STOP cutting the grass, DON'T improve the site and, most controversially, DON'T cultivate the ground.

Bare, disturbed ground is a rarity in Nature. Usually the soil is covered either with vegetation or a mat of decomposing material. Gardeners, inadvertently, spend a lot of time creating the ideal conditions for plants such as groundsel, chickweeds, knotweeds and poppies.

Don't weed.

If the purposes of a garden is useful production, very few sites are ideal. So we strive to make them ideal in a process known as Messification by amending and fertilising the soil, digging, draining, watering, weeding and pruning. Most plants appreciate this treatment by growing bigger and better but these conditions are rare in nature.

Eyebrows might be raised at his next paragraph for Wiltshire is one of the most tidy-minded counties in southern England, particularly recently with the invention of the leaf blower, the strimmer and the sit-on mower. So I don't think many other Wiltshiremen will be following Harper's next piece of advice which was: 'DON'T REMOVE JUNK'.

The complex structure of mixed junk and unsightly old furniture provides a fine range of species and microclimates suitable for homes and hunting grounds for wild animals.

To overcome the problem of how ugly it looks, combine
scattered junk into one or two large piles, cover with
brushwood and simultaneously plant fast-growing
annual scramblers and perennial climbers like ivy
and roses.

DON'T GET RID OF DECOMPOSING GARDEN WASTE.

Another reflex of conventional garden is that decay is
unhealthy and must be sanitised but for the wildlife
garden decay is essential and the cornerstone of the
good chain. Therefore don't remove spent growth.

I am therefore doing very different things in my garden than what my neighbours are doing. Someone has described me as 'being involved in restoration ecology', which I would consider accurate. I warm to the idea of the bioregion. By my shrewd detective work and years of initiation, I have gained some idea of the kind of natural vegetation and wildlife that might have occupied my garden before it was developed hundreds, perhaps thousands, of years ago.

Restoring the original habitat is not easy work. Human settlement has often changed the land so profoundly that the original habitat and community of organisms have changed beyond recognition.

My aim can be summed up like this. I wish to return my whole acre into 'a twisted marshy morass', which is exactly how the hunter-gatherers might have found it before the advent of farming and the Neolithic revolution.

As for tree planting, people think this is wonderful,

but for various reasons it is not. Richard Mabey, who has thought about tree planting the most, says that the practice has a lot to do with guilt. And just as with white saviour complex, landowners have been partly motivated by guilt and partly by having the godlike power to create and then the satisfaction of watching their handiwork come to fruition.

However, few of us have the skills of Capability Brown. Mistakes include not just the famously offensive leylandii hedges, which have ruined lives nationwide, but also avenues of beech trees, often planted with the most noble of intentions to sequester carbon in their leaves, but end up with benighted villages suffering from darkness at noon as these light- and view-hogging trees reach for the skies unless they are severely curtailed in their youth, in which case they can make an agreeable hedge. Once a tree has 'got away' then an expensive tree surgeon must be called in.

Right tree right place is the slogan which should be borne in mind. James Lovelock was a great tree planter when he settled in Wiltshire for a considerable period of time and he planted his own acres with trees.

He then moved from Wiltshire, because he felt sickened and repelled by the prairification of that landscape during the excessive years of the Common Agricultural Policy, and he sought pastures new and greener in the heaped-up richness of Devon where the hobbit-friendly landscape makes ploughing all but impossible.

In retrospect he said he wished that he had allowed his Wiltshire lands to regenerate from scratch, in a process called natural regeneration in which trees and shrubs move in, planted mostly by birds, in a well-known succession which has been documented, and you will eventually arrive at 'Climax Vegetation' which, in our temperate countryside is deciduous woodland, and it will get there by itself and what is there, because it has arrived naturally, is probably of more benefit to nature than the artificial groves that we plant.

No writers have written more on the subject of plantations than Oliver Rackham and Richard Mabey. With the deer and muntjac population and the grey squirrel being similarly out of control, some commentators have argued that any tree planting scheme initiated in Britain now is a waste of money since any plantings will be severely compromised. The squirrels will damage the bark of the trees and the deer will nibble them down to the ground. We have the ability to control these species that are doing so much damage to trees but not the political will, although Mary and I have made a conscious effort to eat as much venison as possible, it doesn't help that the average Briton has yet to develop an appetite for its gamey aroma although at a 'poncy' farm shop favoured by the Chipping Norton set in the Cotswolds we recently purchased a venison chorizo sausage.

The Wrong Leaves

GILES:

THE producers of these wrong leaves are the sort of trees that arrive unbidden and not always welcome on railway embankments. No one planted them, yet often they become some of the richest wildlife habitats in our increasingly manicured and sanitised landscape. Along with motorway embankments these areas make up a considerable proportion of what used to be called rough lands.

Rough Lands

GILES:

These can be defined as uncultivated grasslands of which moors, lowland heaths and chalk downland, along with cliff and coastal marshland, represent the best examples of natural vegetation. With their opportunities for walking and picnicking which this kind of country has traditionally provided, all of these are threatened by agricultural intensification, or worse, coniferisation under the greenwashing mantle of carbon offset.

While my own gardening book is in the gestation stage, I shouldn't really mock Joe Suggs's for being a bit basic. 'Plan your borders carefully by putting the taller guys at the back and make sure you plant everything with enough space in between — the label or the information on the packet will tell you ...' Well thanks for that useful tip, Joe and if it gets young people into the fresh air and away from their screens, no one could argue with that.

But I can argue with calling a plant 'guy'. Like boats I assumed garden plants, especially flowers, were female. My first gardening book, the classic, *The Small Garden* by Brig. Lucas Phillips referred to flowers as chorus-girls or ballerinas. Yes I know that some species are divided into males and females and not having one of both means my strawberry tree, for example, has never produced strawberries.

I suspect Joe hasn't twigged yet that he has in effect swapped one addiction for another. In due course I will jot down a checklist (beloved of all gardeners) for the tell-tale signs of gardening addiction.

My Own Gardening Addiction

GILES:

As a fellow sufferer I caught the gardening bug in the 1980s when I got a pocket handkin of land with the tiny cottage in Essex I owned in my twenties.

I knew that gardening was beginning to be a problem because an old friend, Sasha de Stroumillo, whom I had met at Harrow art school, dropped in unannounced (the worst sin in my book, second only to arriving early).

She found me on my hands and knees (in the days before I needed a kneeler) weeding and preparing a new bit of ground for cultivation. I was 'in the zone', my hands moving feverishly over the surface of the Suffolk clay.

Like driving, gardening offers many opportunities to turn on the auto pilot and think through weighty matters, which might be of a personal or international nature, when engaged in one of those mechanical and repetitive chores that allow the mind to freewheel while achieving a sort of existential oblivion that opiates would provide.

How would I know? I have had no experience of opiates but I imagine the sensation may be similar, yet your mind can roam even to the point of rehearsing awkward conversations that you haven't yet had with difficult people, or even reflecting on examples of *esprit de l'escalier*, things you could have said if you had had the presence of mind, while all the time improving the soil and making it more 'friable', i.e. loose and uncompacted, and increasing the humus content by adding organic matter.

All too soon Joe Suggs will learn a lexicon of equally annoying garden words like tilth, chitting, vernalisation and bastard trenching, although the latter is getting a bit old hat in the wake of the fashionable No Dig school of gardening, as embraced by Charles Dowding.

When Sasha surprised me, obviously, I did jump to attention but not quickly enough. I was accused of being unfriendly. It was not to be the first time. Even when Royal gardeners Julian and Isabel Bannerman once turned up unannounced in my Wiltshire garden, when I was thinning seedlings, an exacting task which requires concentration, I didn't want to break off from the small and satisfying task that had taken me into the zone, even though there was the prospect of trickle-down knowledge that could benefit a common gardener like me.

It's the change of gear from doing something mindless I find difficult. For Mary, the opposite is true. Having seen her own mother and others become 'slaves' to their gardens in Northern Ireland, Mary observed how quickly they reverted to states of wilderness following the deaths of their curators and turned in a few months into wildlife sanctuaries.

I can attest to this. There are bits of my one acre I have abandoned and can no longer recognise because the animal tracks are different from those paths I laid out originally.

The activity of weeding is one of the most pleasurable and addictive tasks for the beginner, intermediate and advanced gardener. Although the advanced gardener will have recourse to long-handled hoe or cultivator to save their backs.

When I worked in London as an assistant to a ragger dragger, stippler and marbleiser (paint effects were all the rage in the eighties), I couldn't wait to get back to my tiny plot in Essex, with its clay soil so congenial to rose growing.

Essex is much maligned, but its flat, unassuming countryside and characterful villages and pubs can still bewitch and enchant. How many fine products can this county boast? The affordable luxury – Maldon sea salt, Colchester oysters, Tiptree jams and conserves to mention but a few.

Its reputational damage owed more to its proximity to the East End of London whose residents, many of whom were cultural fans of the Kray twins, moved out when they were displaced by 'foreigners'.

Mary has been to Jaywick, one of the most deprived of seaside resorts, only to find that one of its fans is the driftwood bird sculptor Guy Taplin, whose work, like Cezanne's, is so powerful it has spawned a cottage industry of lesser imitators who produce decoy bird sculptures for sale by the yard in mid-market designer shops.

But we moved from Essex when Mary decided it was too far from my cottage to her office in London (two and a half hours each way) and relocated to Pewsey which, in those days, had a train service which took only 59 minutes between here and Paddington.

My mother was a Soil Association member. It was she who, during the seedtime of my soul (Wordsworth), first sowed the doubts in my mind that all was not well in the green and apparently pleasant land. Rachel Carson's *Silent Spring* had first alerted her to the fact that the so-called improvements in the world of agriculture, i.e. using pesticides which were a by-product of the medical experiments that had been used by the Nazis in World War II, were actually 'waging war with nature'.

My own membership of the Soil Association would put me on a collision course with most countrymen. It all made sense, but we were seen as crackpots in the seventies and eighties.

Prince Charles talked to plants. Lyall Watson, author of *Supernature*, discovered that plants could respond to music and could feel sensations. Trees could release dormant pheromones to discourage attacking pests.

Watson's findings no doubt paved the way for Peter Wohlleben and the current consensus that forest trees are sentient and support each other through a network of subterranean connections. A system perfectly attuned, according to James Lovelock, to the maintenance of the earth through interactions and feedbacks. Fungi and their mycorrhizal connections, as described in Merlin Sheldrake's book on the subject, *Entangled Life*, have suddenly opened up a new frontier of research and promise for healing a damaged planet. These include the likely possibility of finding a fungus that can digest plastics.

Healing damaged land, that's what I've been doing all these years by providing micro-habitats for critters and birds and over-wintering invertebrates. Industrial agriculture driven by the Common Agricultural Policy has been hammering the environment for decades. Pesticides including fungicides have unleashed a tsunami of problems for the earth system. Agricultural run-off has been identified as the prime suspect in the pollution of Britain's rivers but the 'polluter pays' principle has not yet been properly put into force.

One of the reasons that organic food costs more is that the organic grower will say that they have 'absorbed these externalities'. In other words, it is much harder to farm or garden without chemicals.

One of the most inspiring writers of the early organic movements was H.J. Massingham. In a revealing passage in *The Wisdom of the Fields* (1945), he is only too aware of the brickbats aimed at those who aspire to the organic life. It is said of those who advocate the cultivation of the earth by good husbandry that they are 'warped by nostalgia' and 'cramped by traditionalism', that in their desire to 'keep farming free of all taint of commercialism and industrialism' they 'grope about in a sort of medieval twilight towards a mystical state of which the symbols are the maypole and the night-soil cart'.

How could anyone argue with the noble task of restoring balance and biodiversity to the previous monoculture of wheat that I inherited as the unfeasibly large 'garden' that came with the cottage, towards whose transformation the district council awarded me a tree-planting grant?

Will immersion in his own garden cause Joe Sugg to believe himself to be a 'deep ecologist', having deep thoughts on the lines of 'as above so below'?

Not surprisingly I resent being interrupted from coppicing hazel to take non-driver Mary to Devizes for her routine mammograms.

It never occurred to me to ration the amount of time I spent in the garden. When questioned, I would be defensive. 'I am maintaining the property,' I said.

She grumbled that I spent every hour in the garden and she had married an artist not an unsalaried groundsman. But where was the art?

There was a time when I used to have to drive to Anglesey and stay for a week with my mother. This was not because I was a mother's boy but because it was the only place I could work on my paintings or finish difficult ones requiring maximum concentration. In Wiltshire, I would be tempted into my garden by the green and the ease with which I could slip though the French windows.

Clearly, I was addicted because although for some years I was able to finish the paintings in Anglesey, I then gave in to the addiction and wandered into my mother's garden instead. Mary's fears were realised when I started to garden – and garden with intent – in my mother's walled plot and, as she got older, my mother needed more and more help from her eldest son to clip the bay and the yew into various geometric shapes. So the painting was put on to the back boiler as I went from my own garden on a busman's holiday to my mother's.

The task of shaping my mother's evergreens into giant obelisks, bells, pyramids and balls was made easier by my brother's birthday present of a Henchman tripod ladder. Let's hope Joe Sugg doesn't discover it. It allows the topiarist to work at some slight distance from his object like a sculptor, chiselling away, instead of leaning the ladder on the object. The results, therefore, were stupendous and 50 per cent more accurate than the previous hit-and-miss affair. Even though my mother has sold her property, I am tempted to return in the winter to see if the new incumbents have kept up the extremely high standards that I attained during her last years there.

But gardening should not take over your life. To sum up, although Cedric Morris managed to combine work and painting in the honourable tradition of the painter/plantsman, most artists with gardens have not.

Gardening presents an especially dangerous trap not just for artists but also, it has emerged following lockdown, for others trying to work from home. It is always going to be easier to wander into a garden as a displacement activity rather than thinking.

Accidents and Diseases

GILES:

There is no doubt that gardening is good for your health – until you talk to an A&E nurse. Falls from ladders, allergies to giant hogweed, euphorbia, whose milky sap is toxic to human skin, swallowing dangerous plants (the risk is exaggerated as not many people eat the flowers of foxgloves; nevertheless at a recent wedding I was astonished to see the addition of monkshood – aconitum, one of the most poisonous of our garden plants – in the table bouquets), sprains, cutting through electrical cords with resulting electrocution, standing on a garden rake – the oldest gardening accident of all – and knocking your teeth out, bamboo sticks, which cause grisly eye injuries and are supposed to be always topped with an upturned egg cup, but the gardener was distracted before he got around to it ... Add the need for tetanus jabs or boosters due to cuts from vicious rose bushes and blackberry picking, and I am sure a spokesperson from the Royal Society for the Prevention of Accidents would not agree with Joe Sugg that gardening is necessarily a cure-all.

Before Monty Don was famous he was a jeweller and I met him once at a lunch given by a mutual friend, Catherine Mansel Lewis, near Hay-on-Wye. Monty took the wind out of my sails as he told me off for proselytising. 'We are all organic growers, Giles,' he said. 'But we don't need to beat others over the head about it. And why are you carrying a book on organic growing with you?'

There was an element of truth in what he said because most conventional farmers and growers are trying to navigate an almost impossible bureaucratic system which sometimes seems, they think, designed to trip them up. How often have I heard from farmers, 'We are just trying to make a living. We are not trying to change the world.'

Someone told me that the moment Monty makes any money he will spend it immediately on trees. In his increasingly extensive empire, Mr Don is also clearly a gardening addict and watching his programme *Gardeners' World*, of which I am an avid fan, I couldn't help feeling sorry for him or his assistants, having to clip endless ranks of pointless box pyramids and balls.

Box blight is the latest in a range of plant diseases caused by globalisation that gardeners have to contend with, but box also looks very nice unclipped as it used to grow on hillsides in Surrey.

The shaping and topiarising of evergreen shrubs is another obsession that the gardening addict can fall victim to, as I did while getting 'stuck in' with perfecting those evergreens of my mother's on Anglesey. To some, topiary is an abomination, a distortion of gardening – too much the hand of man and not of nature, rather like the Victorian pastime of using bedding plants to make floral versions of heraldic shields, which could only be seen from the upper storey of the Big House.

Clipping evergreen shrubs into the shape of a locomotive or Marge Simpson is not what gardening is meant to be about. It also means the topiarist can never relax in a deckchair to enjoy the garden as he or she will always have to jump up to correct some imperfection. As for my own topiary efforts at my mother's house, I tended to go for simple peaks or curves.

This leads me, like the ancient mariner, to point out to Joe Sugg that he needs to be careful of becoming a slave to his garden. It might be too late already for Joe, as it is for my brother and to a lesser extent my sister, who have both taken on gardens that have got on top of them.

There would be no problem with my gardening my life away if I had a private income or if the time spent on gardening didn't rob me of the time and life force I could be directing towards realising my talents in the creative field rather than in my own one-acre field.

Restricting the Addiction

MARY:

If I could have one wish it would be to have a personal trainer-type figure in our lives – someone whose authority would genuinely frighten Giles, who would come in the early morning and simply escort Giles to his studio or into the landscape with his paints and make him work for four hours on pain of physical punishment if he tried to stop painting before the time was up. He couldn't do more than four hours because of food-greed issues. Giles is my favourite artist and his gardening addiction breaks my heart. I don't understand why there isn't a support group for gardening addicts and the families of gardening addicts. I believe this is because gardening has yet to be recognised as an addiction.

GILES:

My sister, who is not a wild gardener, is shocked by how quickly nature undoes her handiwork as soon as her back is turned. She tries to practise ex-Mayor Rudy Giuliani's zero tolerance policy. Noting that 'it starts with one weed and soon nettles will be everywhere and an even more pernicious weed, the bindweed, will use the nettle as a climbing frame and gain access to every corner of your garden.' And don't get me started on the dreaded ground elder, which saps the strength of all your garden plants.

Once Mary insisted that I attend a marriage guidance counselling session with her (it was free – the taxpayer paid, back in the days before the government gave up on trying to preserve the traditional family).

I told the woman counsellor that I spent every waking hour of every day in the garden.

'Is this true?' the counsellor asked of Mary.

Mary said yes.

The counsellor told me, 'We would all love to spend every hour of every day in our garden, if we are lucky enough to have a garden – but most people have to attend to work or business. Do you not set any boundaries for yourself?'

I looked blank and grinned amiably like Benny from *Crossroads*. This has always been my default reaction (and Boris Johnson's, by the way) when being attacked by womenfolk.

I wonder, if I'd had a huge private income or a trust fund to underpin these lost man-hours in my garden cutting, slashing, thinning, coppicing, pollarding, hoeing, raking and mulching, would Mary have accepted it then? But she firmly believes in the parable of the talents. She believes that I am a talented artist and that it is a crime to ignore these higher faculties, which leave some imprint in the warp and weft of time, apart from nettles and bindweed.

These decades in the garden, although they help me from turning into Pavarotti, as gardening exercises so many parts of the body and may lower blood pressure, are no substitute for a cottage whose walls are not lined with the fruits of my artistic labour.

'What will there be to show for your life if you don't get on with painting your commissions? Just a field full of rank weeds giving habitat to a muntjac,' says Mary.

Most gardening articles like Joe's end with a quick-glance checklist of bullet points for jobs to do in the forthcoming weeks. For any novice gardener, my checklist would be a series of warning signs pointing to the various degrees of gardening addiction and at the top of that list of problem addiction would be taking on an area too big to manage without paid assistance, which is the situation for many gardeners.

But it depends on your circumstances. Mary knows a man who followed the Grateful Dead for most of his early adulthood. When he came to his senses in his late thirties it was too late for him to mount the career ladder. Fortunately his parents had a sprawling acreage in the Cotswolds and he set to work transforming it into an award-winning garden. His family couldn't be happier that he is in the garden 16 hours per day.

Verge Cutting

GILES:

Alarm bells should ring if and when a gardener starts to cultivate the verges or wayside beyond the curtilage of their property. This sometimes reflects an impulse in an addicted gardener who has run out of things to do in their own garden. Unless said gardener has 'adopted' the verge, in a quest to get more garden to cultivate, the wayside officially belongs to the council so their action may be illegal.

One man's (my own) perception of the beauty of a neglected verge is, of course, another man's vision of chaos, disorder and low village morale. But self-appointed verge tidiers are an ecologist's nightmare. Our native plants have grown up in an ecological relationship with our native invertebrates and birds can suffer at the hand of garish garden-centre plants which strike the wrong note. Town and county councils are often guilty of planting daffodils in the centre of dual carriageways and on motorway roundabouts where they certainly don't belong and most succumb to the salt damage. Incidentally another manifestation of gardening addiction is the practice of tying spent daffodil leaves into knots, a practice I found one gardener engaged in as we looked around on the day his garden was open to the public. But then this was a man who had also taken the Advanced Driving Test, not for any professional reason but because the conventional driving test had been not enough of an ordeal for him, so perhaps he was a glutton for punishment.

Edible Flowers

GILES:

When you find edible flowers in the salad bowl you know the gardener of the house is trying to tell you something, e.g. don't keep me too long at the table, I've got work in the garden to do.

Set Boundaries

GILES:

Gardeners need to set boundaries on all their activities. I have learned too late that the time I might have spent teaching my children to play French cricket or catch a ball can never be won back. All too soon your children will be off to university and, if you are lucky, you will see them at Christmas and Easter. Hence you may regret the time that you spent doing 'important' jobs such as deadheading cosmos in order to promote fresh flower growth and neglecting your children.

MARY:

Thirty years ago we moved to the country – a sacrificial act on my part so my husband and child could enjoy a more natural life, even though at the expense of my own love of socialising. One of us has got lost in the garden but, even so, as Georgia Coleridge observed, when she came to spiritually cleanse the cottage, 'this garden has an exceptionally good healing energy'.

Conclusion

MARY:

I have written as a woman with near insatiable social needs, who can't drive and who has been exiled these last three decades to a village without a bus service.

Commuting is necessary if you need to stay in the swim for professional reasons, but it's physically arduous. I've just weighed my bag of essential items for one overnight trip to London and it was a stone. On the other hand, the train is the only time you get any peace to read.

But the last train back to the exile leaves Paddington at 21.04 and, although I've got friends to stay with in London, it means that over the years I've missed at least six hundred key parties, gallery openings and book launches, to say nothing of memorial services and lectures and art exhibitions. And masses of work in the boom days of journalism when editors rang your mobile wanting to commission you to write a highly paid piece but gave up if they couldn't get through immediately. There used to be never a signal to speak of in our cul-de-sac village.

But Giles lives for nature and so do most children, so I put them first and spearheaded the escape to the country. In those days, I wanted Giles to be happy, but looking back it might have been better for him *not* to have had an acre of land to constantly tempt him away from the easel. Had he been in the Battersea four-room terrace, which was our alternative to rural living, he might have painted to create the landscapes on canvas that he was starved of in real life.

But country life was indisputably better for our children. Moreover, they had a longer childhood.

One twelfth birthday party has stuck in my mind because there were two nymphet girls there, cousins of the host child. These had naked midriffs, dyed hair and – more pertinently – breasts. 'They're only twelve, too,' explained their aunt. 'But girls mature earlier in London.

'It's partly all the oestrogen in the London water and partly because London children look at screens all day because it's too difficult for their parents to keep driving them to the park.'

I liked it that my then twelve-year-old was still childish. After all, if she was going to live to a hundred, that's 82 years of adulthood. No need to fast forward the condition.

There's nowhere to play outside in London, but here the children had dog-walking on the downs, bluebell woods, river swimming, bicycling in the lanes, sandpits, bucket baths (the poor man's hot tub) hammocks, swings, barbecues, a teepee built by Giles from his own willow fronds, skating on frozen puddles, crackling log fires, roast chestnuts and cob nuts from his own trees, and an outdoor 'museum' displaying fossils, hand-worked tools and iron pyrite nodules which we stumbled across in the ploughed fields. Moreover, they had seasons, in the days when there were seasons.

Gap Years were a problem because they'd been brought up in a village where every grown-up man was nice and you'd been into his house and there was a prevailing sense that the whole of life was cosy.

To conclude. The country was better for the children's childhood. Giles would have done more paintings if he had needed to create a beauty spot rather than just stand in one admiring it. I liked having more space than I would have had in London. And Giles has been happier here, even if less productive. Also, I suppose I've had a few laughs at home, even if I've missed out on the socialising.

Yet, I'm certain that a London dwelling would be the best choice for the final decade of life. With the best will in the world, it's too much of a nuisance to visit someone who lives in the country, no matter how much you love them. Yet our friends and family are always in London occasionally and would be 20 times more likely to come and see us there, not least because we could offer them somewhere to stay.

Had we bought that Battersea mid-terrace it would by now have come right. But through living in the country for thirty years we have lost the chance of even a broom cupboard in Battersea.

GILES:

It suddenly came back to me – a conversation when I had just left art school and was 'painting and decorating' the house of a couple of likeable alcoholics of the sort who used to be able to afford to live in Chelsea. The female was an empathetic literary type. The male edited an obscure magazine called *Behind Times*, a quarterly journal for those who indulged in enemas for the express purpose of sexual gratification.

I was then on the cusp of buying a mid-terrace rural slum cottage in Essex for £14,000.

'Don't,' they both said. In fact, they implored me.

'You will become depressed,' said one.

'Especially in the winter,' said the other. 'And if you stay too long in the country you will become alcoholic like us.'

They laughed immoderately before one of them added, 'Oh and you will lose all your charm and frivolity and become really serious and probably start boring on about the Soil Association.'

Cue more laughter, as another champagne cork hit the ceiling I had just finished painting.

I confess that I have become a bore about the Soil Association. I have seen soil erosion with my own eyes, washing off the fields and into drains during high rain events and blowing away into the upper atmosphere during harvesting and ploughing and it doesn't just come back down again. It blows out of the area, but I am surrounded by other bores with different agendas.

The countryside, since that conversation some decades ago, has become something of a parody of itself, beset by Gilbert-and-Sullivan-type rival groups – off-roaders versus ramblers, kayakers versus fly fishermen, Fearghal Sharkey against the water authorities, Amazon delivery vans against child cyclists, hunts against antis, weekenders against church bells and crowing cocks.

The voices are getting shriller.

Yet there have been some improvements in agri-environment schemes – though these are still at the stage of window dressing.

However, someone has given me a book on Regenerative Agriculture and, although I am wary of becoming a man with a mission (look where that got Tony Blair with his WMD), I have a new spring in my step. I am no longer alone in my interest in soil. The subject has become mainstream.

The author of *Dirt to Soil* is Gabe Brown. He makes the point that most arable farming is based on the drenching of the soil with glyphosate, and glyphosate is an antibiotic, so how could it be good for your soil, or your gut? Whatever is the question, he asserts, 'Soil is the answer'.

Finally, I see the green shoots of a possible agricultural renaissance – there could be a farming revolution just around the corner. One where wildlife friendly sustainable farming based on sound ecological principles, which restore rather than degrade soil biota, become the norm.

A new subsidy system could be skewed towards regenerative farming and a very simple test employed to identify the deserving recipients. I can envisage a future where parties of schoolchildren are invited by farm managers to enter the fields with buckets and spades to check for the presence of the humble earthworm. Those who cannot demonstrate their widespread presence, risk forfeiting their pay-outs. Those who can, will receive the endorsement of these earnest mini-Gretas, who would tick-box the green light for the next round of tax-payer's largesse.

Yes, I know I sound like a born-again outsider in the long-running radio series about country life, *The Archers*. In the words of E. O. Wilson, 'there can be no purpose more inspiriting than to begin the age of restoration reweaving the wondrous diversity of life that still surrounds us'.

Acknowledgements

GILES:

I would like to thank Richard Ingrams for giving me a column on *The Oldie* magazine on the very day that I was sacked from *Saga* magazine during my early years of struggle.

I would like to thank Craig Brown (the football manager) for help and inspiration over the years.

I would like to apologise to my younger brother Pip for forcing him to watch *Quatermass and the Pit* at an inappropriate age.

I would like to thank Peter Purves, John Noakes and Valerie Singleton for giving my childhood a sense of added purpose.

Finally, as a keen screen addict, I would like to praise the work of Rodney Bewes, Dinsdale Landen, Peter Vaughan (from *Straw Dogs*) and finally James Purefoy for his performance in the much under-rated science fiction film *John Carter*.

MARY:

I would like to thank all the kind friends and neighbours who have given me, a non-driver, lifts around the country over the years.

Above all we would both like to thank Lorna Russell of Ebury for her wisdom, her benign bossiness and her patience, our agent Julian Alexander for his idea for the book and Harry Mount of *The Oldie*, a great encourager.